POWER
AND INTIMACY
IN
RELATIONSHIPS

THE BALANCED FORMULA FOR SUCCESS

by

John Lucas

TABLE OF CONTENTS

"If there is a book that you want to read, but it hasn't been written yet, you must be the one to write it." — Toni Morrison

Acknowledgements

I want to thank all of the people that have poured part of themselves into my life. I am thankful for such a wonderful and supportive family growing up as a little boy. I am ever thankful for Mr. and Mrs. "I" for being so influential to me when I was an adolescent. I want to thank the pastors at Emmanuel Faith Community Church, including Richard Strauss, for the positive influence they gave me as a young man. I am also thankful for the teachers at Biola University and Talbot Seminary for their influence in my education. I want to thank Chuck Swindoll for his input into my life while I attended Evangelical Free Church in Fullerton, Ca. I am also grateful to Jim Carnevale for his insights into psychology and counseling while I studied at San Diego State University.

I want to thank my editor, Heidi Walker for her input and patience with me. I am also indebted to Bob and Emmeline Taylor for loving me like their own son and giving me such a wonderful gift in their daughter Kimberly who has been a caring and supportive wife for twenty-five years. I have been so blessed by my kids for the love and joy they have given me. I am also grateful to all my clients who have helped me be a better therapist and who have taught me more and more about the importance of power and intimacy in a person's life.

John Lucas

The book website: powerandintimacy.com

John's website: lighthousecounselingservices.org

POWER
AND INTIMACY
IN
RELATIONSHIPS

THE BALANCED FORMULA FOR SUCCESS

Chapter 1

THE KEY TO HAPPINESS: POWER AND INTIMACY

God blessed them; and God said to them, "Be fruitful and multiply, and fill the earth, and subdue it." (Gen. 1:28)

I loved Indiana Jones when I was a child. Looking for treasures and lost secrets, that was me. When the movie "National Treasure" came out, I found my all-time favorite movie. How fun to unlock lost secrets and solve the puzzles of life! When I was a little boy, my family took a trip to Mammoth Caves in Kentucky. So many trails and small caves, what an adventure for a little guy like me. Growing up in South Florida, we would go to the beach, and there were always trails to wander and explore. I grew up with the Hardy Boys books and would read and read. I can still remember the movie "Journey to the Center of the Earth." I love investigating!

Despite the wonders of exploring the natural world, one of the biggest adventures for me as an adult has been to find, not the secrets of caves and hills, but the secrets to healthy relationships. Being a family counselor, I have seen many couples and individuals frustrated in their ability to relate to and respond to one another. If I could only find something to unlock the key, an answer for the people I saw every day. Not only did I stumble upon the secret to healthy relationships, I also found a perfect fit between psychology and Christianity.

When I was going to graduate school, I was lucky enough to find part of the lost secret of relational success, although didn't realize it fully at the time. The discovery came through Dr. Jim Carnevale, the guru of the school, whom I was fortunate enough to get to know and follow closely. One day in class, he gave us the golden key to successful living. He told us how all of psychology can be seen as falling under two umbrellas: power and intimacy. I wondered . . . could it really be that these two keys are all that people need to be happy? It seemed simple, but what did it really mean? Could I find any other confirmation?

Over time, I began to see clients daily who were not happy with their marriages and their lives. As I listened to their complaints, it all started sounding very familiar. "I don't feel he listens to me." "He doesn't care about me." "We're just not connected anymore." "I don't feel valued." "She doesn't really trust me or respect me." "I'm afraid he's cheating on me." Over time, I began to see how my mentor's words might help these families. I could see how these principles would help in relationships with children as well. "He's out of control." "He has no purpose or drive." "She just doesn't seem to care!" I began to realize that the whole focus of their problems was centered on the very two things Dr. Carnevale had discussed in class years before: power and intimacy.

Before I went to graduate school, I had become very interested in Christianity and the Bible. To my surprise, there tucked away in the oldest writings of our day was the same key to successful relationships: power and intimacy. "Be fruitful and multiply, and fill the earth [intimacy], and subdue it [power]." From the beginning, the Creator designed us to be creatures whose purpose in life is to live out power and intimacy. I was lucky enough to find this key due to cross-exposure. One message from psychology and one from Christianity. The two integrated perfectly.

Let's look further at what that means. What do you think of when someone says "power"? I think of safety, security, freedom, respect, creativity, influence, order, and stability. What about intimacy? This is a more complex concept. In this context, I think of feeling connected with another or others. It is a sense of belonging. It is a sense of caring and being cared for. It can be described as having an emotional attachment or bond with another with a sense of acceptance. Intimacy creates a sense of purpose. Without people, life has no purpose. If you were the only person on earth, what would be the point of living? Intimacy is a puzzle that many people have trouble putting together. Yet it is such an important factor in our lives. Without it, life can seem miserable.

Below I have listed a few terms under the broader concepts of power and intimacy that seem to describe the idea of each.

Think of them as describing a healthy "emotional diet plan" representing certain "foods" that are important for a balanced meal.

POWER	INTIMACY
SAFETY	RELATIONAL INVOLVEMENT
SECURITY	UNITY
FREEDOM	ACCEPTANCE
RESPECT	BELONGING
HONOR	TRUST
ACHIEVEMENT	FELLOWSHIP
SUCCESS	EMOTIONAL ATTACHMENT
SURVIVAL	CARING AND BEING CARED FOR
CONTROL	PURPOSE
TRUSTWORTHINESS	FAITH
CREATIVITY	LOVE
COMPETENCY	VULNERABILITY

Psychologists focus on different aspects of life in an effort to understand successful living, but at some point, you'll find that many are focused on the same things: power and intimacy. Friedrich Nietzsche and Alfred Adler focused on power. Most of us are very familiar with Nietzsche's quote, "What does not kill me makes me stronger." John Bowlby, with his attachment theory, focused on intimacy. Daniel Perlman talks about the importance of intimacy, too. Writing in *Canadian Psychology* he states, "Humans have a universal need to belong and to love which is satisfied when an intimate relationship is formed."

Power and intimacy are the building blocks of self-worth. If we have power and intimacy, we feel good about ourselves. We are happy and successful. We have the capability to thrive. These are the easily hidden and overlooked things that are found in the book of Genesis as it describes the beginning of mankind.

> God created man in His own image, in the image of God He created him; male and female He created them. God blessed them; and God said to them, "Be fruitful and multiply, and fill the earth, and subdue it; and rule over the fish of the sea and over the birds of the sky and over every living thing that moves on the earth." (Gen. 1:27, 28)

Be fruitful. This is relational, or alluding to the concept of intimacy. *Subdue the earth.* That certainly sounds like an exercise of power, doesn't it? Man was given a garden to tend (power). He was allowed to name the animals (power). At the very beginning of creation, God's master design was for us to enjoy this sense of empowerment. But it was also decreed: "It is not good for man to be alone" (intimacy). We were designed to be relational. We were made in the image of God, male and female. Together, man and woman represent the image of God. Is God powerful? Most of us would say yes. Is God intimate? Absolutely. It is no wonder that we have these qualities indelibly pressed into our beings. Both men and women need power and intimacy.

The importance of maintaining a healthy balance of power and intimacy leads to what I call the six keys to relational success.

Key #1: Men and women need power and intimacy in their lives to be happy and fulfilled. Have you ever come across someone who seems to have a good dose of both power and intimacy? I can think of a few. I have one friend, a doctor, who exudes them equally. On one hand, he has accomplished a lot. He has studied and has a noteworthy profession. He owns a thriving practice. Yet he also spends time with his family and donates a lot of his free time to help others. One day, when my wife was in the hospital with back spasms, he came to the hospital on his day off and helped her to walk. Not only did he exude happiness and fulfillment, but I would have lunch with him in a heartbeat! People who reflect the qualities of power and intimacy are very attractive. We generally see them as very worthwhile people and want to be around them.

Key #2: These ideas, though necessary, are oppositional. Power has to do with not being hurt. Intimacy has to do with the willingness to be open to being hurt. The two are like oil and vinegar in the salad of life. We need them both, but they don't mix well together. The more you increase your power, the less intimacy you have. There is an inverse relationship between the two. They are, as psychologists like to say, complementary.

The character of Scrooge in *A Christmas Carol* knew this well. As a youngster, Scrooge lost his mother and was left by his father in a boarding school while the other children went home for Christmas. He decided that people just hurt too much. Intimacy was too painful. On a power scale of 1 to 10, Scrooge was a 10. He went after money, safety, and security. On the scale of intimacy, he was a 0. He had no friends. What are your power and intimacy numbers? Everyone has a different combination. Some people are like Scrooge, with high power numbers. Others are on the other extreme—they might have little power but are overflowing with intimacy. They sacrifice themselves for the sake of others. On a scale of 1 to 10, they would be a 10 on intimacy and a zero on power. Such people are overly vulnerable. We might call them doormats or class clowns. They have no protective boundaries or respect from others. People are constantly taking advantage of them. Think about George

McFly in "Back to the Future." George had no value from others and didn't feel he could accomplish anything. He was constantly being picked on by Biff, the school bully, until he finally stood up for himself and found confidence. In doing so, George found more safety and security. He became empowered!

There are a lot of power and intimacy combinations out there. Let's call them P/I combinations. Throughout this book, we will use power as the first number in this formula. Thus Scrooge would be 10 / 0 (10 on power and 0 on intimacy). George McFly would be 0 / 10 (0 on power and 10 on intimacy). Others might be 9 / 1 or 8 / 2 and so on, all the way down to 3 / 7 or less, which would be headed toward the doormat range. Below is a chart on how these numbers correlate with each other. We'll see why this is so important in just a moment.

POWER/ INTIMACY (COMBINATIONS)

(The more of one means the less of the other ↑↓)

P	I
10	0
9	1
8	2
7	3
6	4
5	**5**
4	6
3	7
2	8
1	9
0	10

Key #3: The ideal life is a balanced life that is a 5/5.
This is *the* biggest point of this book. If you want to understand why people are unhappy and frustrated, this is it. Lack of balance. How many people do we know who spend their lives unbalanced in this formula? We all know people who are heavy on one side and light on the other. People who have a 5 on power and a 5 on intimacy have perfect balance. They are choosing a healthy life. Successful people are those who have let down some walls and let some caring people into their lives (intimacy) but have put up some boundaries and gotten rid of some toxic relationships (power) on the other. There are examples of this in the world around us. Look at your backyard fences. If they were thirty feet tall, we would have a lot of protection (power) but not much intimacy with our neighbors. If we had fences that were thirty inches tall, we wouldn't have much protection (power) but we would probably have more intimacy than we want. Most people choose a height that gives them both power and intimacy in a balanced way. The same is necessary with water or soil. When soil is too acidic or too alkaline, plants do not grow. When soil is neutral, plants can thrive. We see that PH balance in our physical bodies, too. The normal PH balance is a very interesting topic and one which has all kinds of ramifications for our health and well-being.

So it is with the balance of power and intimacy. You could view this scale in the form of a continuum similar to the PH test strips you see at the store. The further you drift from center in either direction, the more out of balance you are. You would be either too high or too low on one side or the other. I have used these concepts as the basis for my therapy approach with great success. I have called this approach, "fundamental therapy" as it focuses on the important or essential nature of both psychology and Christianity.

CONTINUUM

BALANCE

POWER------------------/-------------------/------------INTIMACY

$\leftarrow \rightarrow$

P/I

10/0	9/1	8/2	7/3	6/4	5/5	4/6	3/7	2/8	1/9	0/10

Know: People need both power and intimacy in their lives to be happy and fulfilled.

Consider: Which seems more about who you are, power or intimacy?

Do: Find your power and intimacy number combination. It may help to think about your relationship with a significant other. Give yourself a number combination of power and intimacy that you feel you are with them. If you feel you are more powerful than he or she, you would give yourself a power number above a five. The more powerful you are, the closer to ten you would be. After that, choose the corresponding number on the intimacy scale that would add up to ten. If you are higher on providing emotional intimacy than your significant other, you would start on the intimacy side of the scale and give yourself a number above a five and then give yourself a corresponding power number that adds up to ten.

Chapter 2

POWER AND INTIMACY IN RELATIONSHIPS

"I often say that opposites do attract, and then they attack."

— Dr. Neil Clark Warren

Dr. Neil Clark Warren has built a successful ministry on the idea that similarities are preferable for marital bliss. Indeed, his E-Harmony service has found happiness for many couples. Research tends to support the idea that similarities help contribute to a happy marriage. One of the things I have come to realize, however, is that no matter how similar two people may be, differences are inevitable. The key to a happy relationship may not be an all out avoidance of differences but rather a healthy attitude toward them.

Let me suggest why I believe differences are inevitable. In Eastern philosophy, every yin has its yang. Yin and yang are not thought of as opposing forces but as complementary parts of one whole. In other words, the one helps to define the other. In a way, you cannot have one without the other. I love that concept. This idea of complementary opposites is also expressed in Judeo-Christian ideology. Good has evil, joy has sadness, and love has hate.

When we look at a person we are interested in dating, we may see similarities and differences that attract us, but the key to relational bliss is really found in our *attitude* at the beginning of a relationship. We see someone's similarities and are attracted by the thought that this is someone who shares our values and beliefs. We participate in the same hobbies and take up the same causes. If there are differences, they don't throw us for a loop. In fact, we might see them as things that we, ourselves, are lacking—differences that complement us and would enrich our

9

lives together. We think, "Gee, if I hang around this person, I will grow and add parts of myself that will make me better." When we have a positive attitude, we are usually focused on being in charge of ourselves. When we get into a negative attitude, we are usually focused on being in charge of others.

Unfortunately, once we are in a relationship for awhile, our attitudes can change. Instead of focusing on relational harmony and growth, we start to see similarities as boring or competitive and differences as lonely and oppositional. The similarities become dull and the differences become frustrating. We begin to look at the glass as half empty rather than half full. Chuck Swindol (whom I was lucky enough to have as a pastor while attending Biola University and Talbot Seminary) has some wonderful things to say about attitude. "The longer I live, the more I realize the impact of attitude on life," he writes. "I am convinced that life is 10% what happens to me and 90% how I react to it."

One of the keys to being a good counselor is helping people "reframe" their worlds as described by Virginia Satir. Today it is common to hear people talking about "paradigm shifts," or a whole new way of looking at or doing things. Paradigm shifts happen all the time in the world around us, wouldn't you agree? Guess what that means? It means that it is possible for you and me to have paradigm shifts, too. If your attitude needs to change toward your partner, one of the things that is helpful is to have a paradigm shift—to go back and look at your partner's similarities and differences in a positive way. Be thankful that you have someone who can join you in the same activities or philosophies. Appreciate the differences between you as a way to help you grow and gain some of those qualities yourself.

Every quality has a positive and negative side to it. Allow your partner's differences to be something you go with and gain from. My wife is very relational. She always enjoys being with people. She thrives on close connections and emotional intimacy. I'm more on the power side of the equation. I'm good with boundaries (too good). If it were up to me, I would probably have had one or two children and that would have been it. I would rarely have people over to eat and we would rarely go out. Somehow, I ended up with five children, we have a friend of my daughter's who has lived with us and seems like ours now, and we have two cats and two dogs on occasion. Not only that, but our house is the place to hang out for a lot of our friends. You know what? I love it all. I can either get frustrated with my wife or allow her to influence me to be more caring and relational. Likewise she can get frustrated with me or allow me to help her with her boundaries. It can be a win/win.

From the time I started sharing the power and intimacy formula with my clients, I also began sharing how people not only have their own P/I combinations, but how they can have different combinations in different places. A person could be very powerful at work, like an 8/2, but then go to his mother's house and she bosses him around so he turns into a 2/8. I go on to tell them that I am just as interested in how they are with their spouses. Why do I do that? First I'm a marriage counselor and that's the relationship I'm interested in. Second I find that the marriage relationship is the one that most often accurately describes the true person.

Key #4: We tend to match with our opposite formula. When I work with couples, I give them a sticky pad and ask them to draw the P/I scale and come up with a number combination that they feel represents how they act with their spouse. An interesting thing starts to happen. They put down exact opposite combinations! A man might write down 7/3, while his wife writes down 3/7. There is a reason for this. We tend to attract people who are the inverse of ourselves. If we are a 7/3 on the power and intimacy scale, then we will either attract someone who is a 3/7 or we will influence our current partner to move in that direction in order to get along with us. That is what we call "relational homeostasis." The other person will come into balance with us or we will come into balance with them because we do not want to stay in continual conflict.

For all of us, the healthy goal is 5/5. We want to be healthy and we want our spouses to be healthy. An equal amount of power and intimacy is the healthiest emotional state. Someone with this balance can equally put up boundaries and care about others. This is like soil in the backyard that is not too acidic or too alkaline. It will allow plants to thrive and grow. Jesus is our ultimate example. The more we move toward a 5/5 balance, the more Christ-like we become. If we tend to attract the inverse of what we are living, then if we are 5/5, we will tend to attract partners who are 5/5 as well. That's going to be a well-balanced relationship. If we are off balance, however, this is a much less healthy situation on two levels. First because we want a healthy partner, not an unhealthy one. Second because we will influence others to be the opposite of ourselves and we don't want to influence someone into an unhealthy state.

Key #5: You cannot be out of balance and expect others to provide what you are lacking. If you are out of balance, you are out of balance. Taking from others what you lack only puts the other person out of balance as well. You both become depleted in different areas, and you both will be unhealthy and unhappy. Offering to trade what you are strong in, to get what you are weak in, does not work. That is codependency. Let me give you an example. Suppose you decide you aren't going to buy milk ever again. You decide to just borrow it from your next-door neighbors whenever you need it. Let's suppose your neighbors decide to do the same thing with bread. When they need bread, they will come over and borrow it from you. Can you imagine the problems with that? Suppose your neighbors aren't home when you want milk. Or suppose they are out of milk. Or suppose they buy whole milk and you want nonfat milk. The same thing could happen with bread. Suppose they want whole wheat and you buy sourdough. You might have really liked these neighbors at the beginning because they always had a lot of milk, and they might have liked you because you had a lot of bread. But over time, both families will become increasingly unhappy with the other. The same it is in marriage. Wouldn't it be much better to generate what you need on your own and let the other person do the same? There would be a lot more happiness and less frustration!

We must all learn to provide for our own emotional needs of power and intimacy to be happy and relationally content. Allow the qualities of others to motivate you to growth rather than dependency. Let other people make you a better person, not a bitter person.

Key #6: If you want to fix your relationships, focus on fixing yourself! One analogy that I use quite often is the backyard analogy. This is a tool to help us not become too intimate (over-involved or codependent) or too powerful (under-involved or controlling) and to appreciate the importance of working on ourselves to change our relationships. In this analogy, we all live in a fantasy world in which everyone becomes a house and a backyard. Imagine that I am someone close to you whom you love. We would be next-door neighbors. You look into my yard (or life) and notice that I have a lot of weeds (problems) in it. You, being a kind-hearted and caring person, offer to climb over the fence and help me weed them out. About noon I say to you, "I'm hot and tired. I'm going into my house to watch TV and drink a beer." Now you're stuck weeding my yard while I'm kicking back and relaxing. What's going to happen? You're going to become frustrated and resentful. You wonder why no one is helping out in your yard. You know there must be weeds over there, too, that you haven't had time to pull because you're over in my yard weeding mine. Meanwhile, I'm kicking back and relaxing and get irritated because you bought some tulips and started planting them in my yard. I hate tulips! Nobody wins! I start yelling at you and you throw your hands up and say, "I'm done. I'm going back into my yard and taking care of my own weeds."

Then you do. You put in a water system and trees and flower beds. Your house looks great. Your front yard has beautiful flower beds in it. Your neighbors across the street are very impressed with your yard and are looking forward to being your friend. Three of your neighbors are even putting in flower beds because yours looks so good. In a crazy way, you're having a better impact on your neighborhood and you've never left your own backyard.

This is a life that has a balance of power and intimacy. Working on yourself is changing your world. Meanwhile, you've learned that climbing a fence doesn't work. You've learned that there are a lot better things you could do to influence what happens over there instead. You could encourage me. You could give me a copy of your irrigation plan since your watering system is already in. You could tell me there is a sale on plants at the local hardware store. Now you've become a caregiver, not a caretaker. In a caregiver role, everybody wins. You are taking care of yourself and it is motivating me to do the same. You do not have to neglect yourself to love others. You do not need to ignore others to care of yourself.

At the same time, we need others to respect our yards as well. We need to respect others, but we cannot allow ourselves to be disrespected or allow others to take advantage of us. We'll talk more about this later in the book.

As you work on yourself, you change others. Let's go back to our P/I formula for a moment. If I am a 7/3 and you want to get along with me, you had better be a 3/7. Otherwise, we conflict. As you know, humans will not stay in a relationship of conflict for long. There are only two options if we don't fit: rebalance until we are in harmony or leave the relationship. We must have relational harmony or balance. We must have relational homeostasis.

This is the exciting part. If you are a 5/5 and I am a 7/3, we will have conflict until things balance. If you can maintain a 5/5 balance, guess what? You are not only keeping yourself healthy, you are drawing me into emotional, psychological, and spiritual health, too! Just think about this. All you have to do is focus on keeping yourself healthy and you are drawing me and everyone else you come in contact with into a healthier balance, too. Win/win! This is the beauty of the backyard analogy. You and I don't have to get up every morning and worry about everyone else's backyards. If we want to improve our neighborhoods, all we have to do is work in our own yards.

Many of my past clients are now saying to themselves, "I've got to stay in my own yard to change my world." This is the idea of Jesus' statement in the Sermon on the Mount: "You are the light of the world. A city set on a hill cannot be hidden; nor does anyone light a lamp and put it under a basket, but on the lampstand, and it gives light to all who are in the house" (Matt. 5:14,15). We must not neglect the light. Our job is to keep the light shining. If we focus on taking care of us, we will affect those around us. If the root is good, the fruit is good. A farmer does not spend his time focusing on the branches. He spends his time watering and supporting the tree and its roots. If the farmer does a good job with the root, the result will be fruit. The root of the tree is us and the fruit is our relationships. If we work on us, we will naturally bear good relationships.

One of my favorite movies is "Field of Dreams." I think the reason this movie affects many people in such a positive way is because of this principle. Here was a man who worked really hard in his own cornfield to make something special. Sure, there were a lot of other cornfields, but none had a baseball stadium in them. He had made something so different and attractive that he didn't have to worry what was going on in anyone else's field. His was so attractive that James Earl Jones could say, "Oh, people will come, Ray. People will most definitely come."

Another thought that is helpful to me has to do with the concept of love. I had a client say that his girlfriend broke up with him because she felt hopeless and love never lasts. As he shared this story, I couldn't help but think about that statement. I told him that I thought I had a good response that he might use in the future. Love *does* last forever. It is only people who don't!

I go back to the illustration of a farmer and his crops. Think about the farmer's attitude in working the land. He gets up and tills the ground and seeds it. As the seasons move on, he watches his crop grow. I'm not a farmer, but I imagine he's out there watering the crops and making sure they thrive throughout the seasons. At some point, there comes a harvest and all the work that entails. Finally there is a winter and everything dies. The following year, the farmer goes out and

15

does it all over again. Love is a lot like that. We meet people. We enjoy getting to know them, and we foster the relationship. At some point we move on and repeat the process. I had a lot of great friends in elementary school, but I don't see any of those people now. The same it is with high school. But like the farmer, I go out and enjoy the process. With some people, I'm in spring with them. With other people, I'm in fall. We can have different relationships in different seasons. Who said life was dull? Even in a long-term marriage, there is a time in which one person may pass away. Winter does not take away from the joy and great reward of the rest of seasons.

> There is an appointed time for everything. And there is a time for every event under heaven. A time to give birth and a time to die; a time to plant and a time to uproot what is planted. (Eccl. 3:1–2)

Why not embrace the process and enjoy the moment? One positive way of looking at it is that you get to enjoy the fun over and over again! We don't just get one spring. We get many springs! We get many summers! Lucky us. "You have established all the boundaries of the earth; you have made summer and winter" (Psalm 74:17). Understanding love this way will help us to feel more empowered just as the farmer does, and better able to appreciate intimacy as we understand how love works. Love is always there. Sometimes we are not.

Know: We tend to influence others to complement (match oppositely) our power and intimacy.

Consider: Read Luke 9:12-17. Consider how Jesus used power and intimacy in his ministry with his disciples.

Do: Guess your partner's number combination of power and intimacy and compare your combination to theirs. Perfect opposites have no conflict but may not be healthy. The goal is for each person to get to 5/5. The rest of the book will help you move in that direction.

Chapter 3

POWER DEFINED

"Character is power." — Booker T. Washington

What is power? On the surface, it seems easy to define, but the more I've thought about it, the more interesting the answer becomes. Obviously, power involves existing and staying alive. There can be no more singular need than that. Humans have built within them a survival drive. We have all heard stories of incredible survival. Power, then, includes the ability to meet our own physiological and safety needs. This is exactly what Maslow stated in his hierarchy of needs.

But as Maslow pointed out, we also want to be loved and connected to other people. This takes us back to the beginning of creation: "God blessed them; and God said to them, 'Be fruitful and multiply, and fill the earth, and subdue it; and rule over the fish of the sea and over the birds of the sky and over every living thing that moves on the earth'"(Gen. 1:28). The decree for man was to fill the earth (intimacy) and rule or subdue it (power). Man was put in the garden of Eden to cultivate it and keep it (Gen. 2:15). This carries the idea of working and maintaining the garden. Therefore the decree to man meant three things. One was to subdue, one was to work at something to provide, and one was to keep things orderly and running smoothly.

All of this is an expression of power. We humans have a desire to overcome things. We love a challenge. Just look at all of the different ways we express that. We have wars, we have sporting events, and we climb mountains. We put men on the moon. We like to create or achieve things that have purpose. We build large buildings and wonderful bridges. We like to watch over and take care of whatever we have created. If you have known someone who works on cars for a hobby, you know what

I'm talking about. Some people just love to wash and nurture their cars and are constantly pampering them to keep them in fine working order. I know as a parent I am constantly trying to keep my family running smoothly. Can I pay the bills this month? How am I going to fix that washing machine? I'd better keep an eye on those front tires going bald.

God is the same way. He accomplished the work of creation, and he enjoys the process of maintaining that which he created. He, too, will subdue his enemies. God is sovereign. I love the passage in Isaiah that declares God's sovereignty along with foretelling the coming Messiah. His sovereignty speaks of his power and his declaration of the coming Messiah speaks of his intimacy. "Thus says God the Lord, who created the heavens and stretched them out, who spread out the earth and its offspring, who gives breath to the people on it and spirit to those who walk in it, 'I am the Lord, I have called You in righteousness, I will also hold You by the hand and watch over You, and I will appoint You as a covenant to the people, as a light to the nations'" (Isa. 42:5, 6).

Power, then, is anything that ensures and contributes to my well-being within my environment. It tends to be mostly external in focus, whereas intimacy tends to be mostly internal in focus. I once had a client who had experienced little power for most of her life. Growing up, she had a history of different types of abuse. Her idea of power was having "one over" on another person. She felt frustrated her whole marriage that her husband was too powerful and mean to her. There had been a power struggle throughout most of their relationship. Fortunately, with a lot of hard work, their marriage became positive and enjoyable.

Do you know what she did after that? She opened a credit card and started spending without telling him. She got online and started flirting with an old friend she hadn't talked to in years. She couldn't understand what she was doing. She said, "I don't get why I'm doing this when everything is going so well." It might be tempting to think she was sabotaging things to go back to a more comfortable place. Although this could have been part of the answer, I suggested that perhaps she was doing these things because they made her feel empowered. I could see a light bulb go off in her head. She said that had struck a cord with her. She had not felt empowered most of her life. She admitted she did feel powerful when she did those things. Of course, those things were also detrimental to her intimacy. She was losing relational harmony, unity, and trust. If her husband found out, she would lose all she had worked for: her marriage, her husband's respect, and her family security. Her idea of power was tainted.

She did not consider that her empowering actions affected her need for intimacy. She thought power meant dominating another person. This is very typical. Many people on the power side believe dominance over another is the ultimate goal. She also believed that power was doing whatever she felt like doing, whatever felt good. If you go back to Maslow's hierarchy of needs, it becomes a lot more clear what healthy power is about. We need to start with the basic physiological and safety needs, but we follow that with the need for love, belonging, and esteem. Healthy power is about power with an eye open to the importance of intimacy. Healthy power is power that helps me exist and sustain life as well as promote intimacy (emotional bonding). Any exercise of power that detracts from that is not constructive power.

Booker T. Washington, an American educator and leader of the African-American movement in the post-Civil-War era, is a prime example of healthy empowerment. In his lifetime, he was able to effect great change due to his ability to maintain relationships with leaders of the country. He had a power network of supporters his opponents called the "Tuskegee Machine," but Washington maintained power, not because of the Tuskegee Machine, but because of his ability to gain the support of a wide variety of leaders regardless of race or background. He was supported by influential whites, leaders in the black business community, leaders in the educational and religious communities, philanthropists, and politicians on both sides of the aisle. He realized how important character is in the ultimate goal of safety and security. Character is something that affects intimacy. By saying that character is power, Washington stumbled across this lost formula and used it to become a major success in his day. He was able to go on and make huge impacts in the fields of education, politics, and financial improvement for African Americans and wrote fourteen books in the process. For him, power was veiled in the importance of intimacy. He had a healthy blend of power and intimacy—an "iron fist with a velvet glove."

The woman I had seen in my office had let her feelings get in the way of making healthy choices. How many of us can relate to that? It seems as if we are constantly tempted to do what feels good. In a way, we are tempted to do what feels like power or what feels like intimacy, even if it actually brings less of either one (or both). One metaphor that has helped me and some of my clients in the area of healthy decision-making is living life as if you were sitting at a train crossing. As the train comes by, imagine it is divided into three parts: the engine, the middle cars, and the caboose. The engine is your mind. It includes your will, what you decide to do. It is an expression of information you have acquired and the course of action you decide to take. The middle cars are your behaviors, which follow the engine. The caboose is your feelings that result from those behaviors.

Let's put the train to the test. The doctor shows you x-rays that appear to show lung cancer. The engine has new information and you make the intellectual decision to quit smoking. As we sit in the car and watch the train go by, the only thing that has passed by is the engine. You've made a decision to quit. You still smoke, and while some psychologists would argue this, you still feel like smoking. But after awhile, you work on stopping those behaviors and eventually you do quit. Now the middle cars have gone by. But you may still feel like smoking. Eventually, your feelings will change. The caboose will follow the rest of the train if you allow it to do so. Another example is that you decide to get up early and go to the gym and work out. (By the way, you're a better person than me if you do!) You've made a decision, yet you haven't done it yet (behavior), and you really don't feel like doing it either (feelings). But you go anyway (behaviors following the decision). Eventually, you feel good that you went, but it is usually the last thing on the list.

Where people get into trouble is when they allow their feelings to dictate their actions. Just imagine if you woke up and felt like staying in bed, so you didn't go to work. Or you felt like hitting someone over the head with a golf club, so you did. That's the danger of putting the caboose in the front of your train.

Here is something else to think about. Guess where those feelings came from? Many times, feelings in conflict with the rest of the train came from a previous train! Now that's something to think about. As we create new train rides, we are creating new feelings (or cabooses) that will in the future invite us to head in a similar direction. That can be promising or foreboding. The woman I mentioned earlier had put the caboose in the front of her train. She was doing things she *felt* brought her power but in reality were damaging her intimacy. Her actions were not ensuring her relational safety. She had worked hard in her marriage to get more power, and when she finally got to a place of equilibrium, she kept going at the cost of intimacy. It is as if the salad had too much vinegar and she kept adding more and more oil and now she has too much. She must quickly fix the salad or she or her husband (or both) may get tired and toss the salad out.

When you look at the nature of God in the Christian framework, it is interesting to see that God the Father is largely described in terms of power. God the Holy Spirit is largely described in terms of intimacy or the relational component. In Jesus Christ, we see the human representation of both. Christians are to become Christ-like in their natures, which is the reflection of the balanced P/I formula.

Some people might surmise that men tend to be more interested in the power side of the equation and women more interested in the intimacy side. In general, that tends to be true. However, as I have talked with many couples, it is apparent that men and women both want power and intimacy. Yes, men tend to value power and women tend to value intimacy, but find me a

21

woman who wouldn't also like some of the qualities of power (such as respect) and a man who wouldn't like the qualities of intimacy (love). Every time I have made that observation to my clients, I have gotten a resounding, "Yes!"

In the New Testament book of Ephesians (5:33), there is a reference to this formula that men do need to be respected (a quality of power) and women do need to be loved (an aspect of intimacy). This supports the idea that men and women tend to enjoy one side more than another, but they are not mutually exclusive. I have asked many couples over the years about their preference, and there does not seem to be an absolute either way. The word "respected" in Ephesians 5:33 is translated that way only once in the Bible. Most everywhere else it is translated "fear." The Greek word used for respect in that verse is where we get our word phobia. I laugh a little at that. Women are to have a phobia for their husbands.

However, the kind of power a woman wants from her husband is not the same word. Men are to "honor" their wives (1 Peter 3:7). That word carries the idea of cherishing and valuing her. This difference is exactly the idea we see in our relationship with God. We respect God as His bride; He honors or values us as a symbolic husband.

David spoke about the power of God while he endeavored to build a temple for God: "Both riches and honor come from You, and You rule over all, and in Your hand is power and might; and it lies in Your hand to make great and to strengthen everyone" (1 Chron. 29:12). God the Father is the one who can bring fear and judgment. As I look through the Bible, I see only one verse connecting judgment with the Holy Spirit. When we look at the Holy Spirit, we see many more references to intimacy. He is the teacher, the gift-giver, and the helper. It is he who unites believers. In Jesus, we see examples of power, but not at the cost of intimacy. "They were all amazed, so that they debated among themselves, saying, "What is this? A new teaching with authority! He commands even the unclean spirits, and they obey Him" (Mark 1:27). Although Jesus expressed strong authority and power while on earth, he was also caring and relational. When

Mary and Martha were so upset by the loss of Lazarus, their brother, "Jesus wept" (John 11:35).

There is another interesting thing about power. Power as we define it is determined to be safety over our environment. It also carries the idea of competency over the difficulties of life. It means to be in charge of something, too. All of this tells me that being responsible for too much can actually contribute not to feeling powerful, but to feeling powerless. In Genesis, notice that man was to be in charge of the garden. He wasn't told to run the universe. He was given a limited amount of authority that he could handle. He was not overwhelmed or he would have been power*less*. One of my favorite movies is "Bruce Almighty." That was exactly the problem for Bruce. He was in charge of too much. He couldn't handle it and kept messing up. By the end of the movie, he felt terrible and wanted his old job back. He wanted to be back in a position of security. Therefore, those people who are able to focus on being responsible for themselves are actually more powerful than those who feel a need to be responsible for others.

Know: God is a wonderful balance of power and intimacy.

Consider: Consider the different ways God expresses his power in the Bible (creativity, judgment, sovereignty).

Do: Note the ways you feel empowered this week.

Chapter 4

INTIMACY DEFINED

"Kissing is very good. But we have something
better." — Neytiri ("Avatar")

What is intimacy? Since intimacy is one of the centerpieces of this book, let's take a moment to clarify what it means. If you were to ask many couples about how they were doing in the area of intimacy, guess what they would say? You guessed it. They would talk about their sex lives. But while sex is an expression of intimacy, intimacy itself is much more complex and intangible.

I like the way Wikipedia defines intimacy:

> Intimacy generally refers to the feeling of being in a close personal association and belonging together. It is a familiar and very close affective connection with another as a result of a bond that is formed through knowledge and experience of the other. Genuine intimacy in human relationships requires dialogue, transparency, vulnerability and reciprocity.

> Intimate relationships play a central role in the overall human experience. Humans have a universal want to belong and to love, which is satisfied within an intimate relationship. Intimate relationships consist of the people that we are attracted to, whom we like and love, romantic and sexual relationships, and those whom we marry and provide and receive emotional and personal support from. Intimate relationships provide people with a social network of people that provide strong emotional attachments and fulfill our universal need of belonging and the need to be cared for.

That's a great explanation. I love the idea that humans have a universal want to belong and love. Mother Teresa was quoted as

24

saying, "The most terrible poverty is loneliness, and the feeling of being unloved."

The fibers of our being have been indelibly etched by God. We have been created to be relational. That's what intimacy is all about. It is more than a connection between two people. It is a sharing of your soul with another person. This definition also tells us what intimacy is not. There are things people do that can be an expression of intimacy but in and of themselves are not intimacy. Sex is an example. The act of sex can be a wonderful expression of love and emotional attachment. However, the act of sex can also be an expression of selfishness and pain. With many of the couples I see, there has been infidelity. Often that infidelity was not a result of emotional intimacy. It was simply a shared pleasure between two people. Sex can be an expression of emotional intimacy, but it is not intimacy.

Submission is another example. When someone willingly chooses to submit to the will or desire of another, especially out of a sense of trust and respect, this can be an expression of intimacy. But like sex, it is not intimacy itself. Submission is a bridge with a possible connection between two people. It can also be offered without any intimacy at all. If you have ever worked with a difficult boss, you know that your submission is in no way emotional intimacy. Or how about the time you were speeding and saw flashing lights behind you? I'm sure you pulled over, but I'm going to guess you wouldn't call that emotional intimacy. So submission can be an expression of intimacy, but it is not intimacy itself.

Acts of love are another example. Showing kindness to someone can be an expression of deep intimacy. At the same time, you and I can go down to any homeless shelter and express the physical act of feeding the poor with no personal connection whatsoever. Acts of love can be expressions of intimacy, but in themselves, they are not intimacy.

When you look at the life of Jesus, you see that he submitted to people he was not intimate with. When Jesus submitted to the guards in the garden of Gethsemane and then to Pontius Pilate, he was not intimate with them. This is an important point. Also, Jesus sometimes often offered acts of love with no connection or intimacy either. There were several occasions in which he healed people with no emotional connection whatsoever. There is no record of those people having any kind of fellowship with Jesus at the time. One example is the guard who had his ear cut off by Peter in the garden of Gethsemane. Jesus healed his ear, but there was nothing said about sharing of intimacy with the guard.

In John 14:22 Judas (not Iscariot), who was one of the apostles, asked Jesus why he was going to disclose himself to the apostles and not to the world. Jesus responded by saying that it is those who love Jesus and keep his words that he and the Father would be intimate with. Jesus had requirements before people could receive the gift of intimacy with him. In John 15, followers of Christ are likened to branches connected to a vine. Jesus says that we must abide in him. We must be emotionally and intimately attached. If we do not remain attached, we can be thrown away and dried up (verse six). Intimacy is earned!

A word used in the Bible to describe intimacy is "fellowship." There is such a nice explanation of this term found in the letter of Philippians penned by the apostle Paul. "Therefore if there is any encouragement in Christ, if there is any consolation of love, if there is any fellowship of the Spirit, if any affection and compassion, make my joy complete by being of the same mind, maintaining the same love, united in spirit, intent on one purpose." That sure sounds like intimacy. Just look at the movie "Avatar." Intimacy flows all throughout that movie. The main character, Jake Scully, very much wants to be part of the family of Na'vi. He works hard to earn that intimacy. In the end, he is included in the family permanently. One of the expressions of that intimacy is the connection of his soul to Neytiri described in the script. "Neytiri takes the end of her queue and raises it. Jake does the same, with trembling anticipation. The tendrils at the ends move with a life of their own, straining to be joined" ("Avatar," 2012).

There is one very important point about intimacy that needs to be mentioned. It is very logical to withhold intimacy when you or I are being wronged by another person. This is not an unhealthy or an un-Christian thing to do. This is consistent both biblically and psychologically. In psychological terms, we call it preventing codependency. The idea is not enabling another person to continue to do wrong with no real consequences. Biblically, it is called "breaking fellowship." When man first sinned, the clear, healthy thing God did was give him consequences. One of those consequences was a loss of intimacy, or fellowship, with him. When Adam and Eve did wrong, their loss of intimacy with God was represented by their banishment from the garden of Eden. Their son Cain felt the full pain of the loss of intimacy, too, when he killed his brother Abel and was sent into exile. Cain said to the Lord, "My punishment is too great to bear! Behold, You have driven me this day from the face of the ground; and from Your face I will be hidden, and I will be a vagrant and a wanderer on the earth, and whoever finds me will kill me" (Gen. 4:13,14). Poor Cain.

But God has been clear that intimacy is earned, and it can be lost. "For the devious are an abomination to the Lord; but He is intimate with the upright" (Prov. 3:32). When Moses said goodbye to the children of Israel as they went into the Promised Land without him, God spoke of the coming day when they would turn from following him altogether. He told them what he would do: "But I will surely hide My face in that day because of all the evil which they will do, for they will turn to other children" (Deut. 31:18). So one very biblical consequence to being selfish and hurtful is to lose fellowship. My clients often say, so what does that mean? To me, that means that you go ahead and make dinner and do the laundry, but you are distant, aloof, and cold. Your words are short and to the point. You avoid any major discussions. You spend time alone. This is not done with a heart of meanness but with an eye towards reconciliation. Isn't God the same way?

I have come across many people in my practice who have a hard time with this. To many people, breaking fellowship with someone does not seem to be the Christian thing to do. However, the Bible is clear that this is what God does with those who are in the family. Breaking fellowship does not mean that believers are no longer in the family of God. It does mean that they are temporarily disconnected from God and from others. It is as if we have unplugged ourselves from God's intimacy, and we are, like Peter during his denial of Christ, hungry to get plugged back in. The apostle John strikes home with this message when he says, "If we say that we have fellowship with Him and yet walk in the darkness, we lie and do not practice the truth" (1 John 1:6). This does not mean that God does not love us. For those who have come into the family of God through faith and repentance, it does not mean you are out of the family. Notice the apostle John says "we" when he talks to those who walk in darkness. "We" refers to believers in Christ. John makes it clear what we must do to get out of the darkness and back into the light. "If we confess our sins, He is faithful and righteous to forgive us our sins and to cleanse us from all unrighteousness" (1 John 1:9).

"If we say that we have not sinned, we make Him a liar and His word is not in us" (1 John 1:10). We must admit and acknowledge our sin to God. We must also love others. "The one who loves his brother abides in the Light and there is no cause for stumbling in him. But the one who hates his brother is in the darkness and walks in the darkness" (1 John 2:10, 11). When my children do wrong, they must come and make it right, but they are still my children. God says as much in that often quoted verse, "If My people who are called by My name will humble themselves, and pray and seek My face, and turn from their wicked ways, then I will hear from heaven, and will forgive their sin and heal their land" (2 Chron. 7:14 NKJV). Notice that God again says, "My people." Even though they have done wrong, they are still God's people. Once they have turned back to God, fellowship is restored! This is what we can do for those we love, too, whether they are friends or children or a spouse. We can withhold fellowship (or intimacy) until it has been earned. I have seen this principle used successfully in many situations in which families and marriages have been restored.

People who are higher on the intimacy scale tend to be more givers than takers. They tend to think more about others than themselves. In a way, intimacy people can be over-givers, while power people are under-givers. Therefore, when you think of ways to help the intimacy person be motivated to change, it must be framed in a way that works with their worldview. Intimacy people would ask the question, so how does this help other people? Power people have a worldview that generally is self-based. They would ask the question, so how does this help me? As a therapist, I must shroud things in a way that motivates people from the perspective of their own worldview. By the way, the healthy question from the balanced person would be, so how does this help me and my neighbor?

Because intimacy people are motivated to change if it helps others, it is reassuring that withdrawing intimacy is a healthy consequence that encourages such people to rebalance their lives and only practice "power" things that also protect intimacy. Destructive behaviors of power throw such people off balance and it is important that they feel the consequences quickly so they can rebalance. Intimacy people quickly see the results of their imbalanced actions. Someone will treat them poorly. Power people must see the consequences of their actions, too. Let's take the example of a little boy at the museum who pulls a bone out of the dinosaur when no one is looking. The whole dinosaur crashes down in a cloud of dust and an explosion of noise. Everyone turns around in shock, and as the boy turns to look at the crowd, you know what he has on his face? He has either shock or sometimes, a smile. Either way, you know what that look means? "I matter. What I do affects others." This consequence brings a sense of self-worth. For this person, life now has meaning and purpose.

Intimacy in its very context means pain. It also means joy. Whenever you open yourself to care about something or someone, you are opening yourself to pain. Pain if the hope you have doesn't come true. Pain if the person you care about dies or suffers or lets you down. To love something means you are allowing the possibility of losing it to hurt you. That kind of pain is not bad pain. Most pain in our experience is negative. But the kind of pain that comes from caring about people is good pain. It means you are giving honor to that person who has earned it. It would be dishonoring not to be hurt by the loss of someone who has made such an impact on your life. I call this the shadow of love. When the sun hits a sundial, it leaves a long streak of brightness. The other side of the sundial is a mirror or shadow of that light. It tends to be as long as the sunlight, but in the other direction. Love is the same way. You can love a little and you will only hurt a little. Or you can love a lot and risk hurting a lot. The choice is up to you. I would rather choose the long shadow. To me, that's living. I love the quote from John Wooden, the great UCLA basketball coach: "Happiness begins where selfishness ends."

In the previous power chapter, marriage was described as a reflection of the relationship between God and mankind. God is seen in the role of the husband, to be respected; believers are seen as the wife, to be honored. It is the same illustration with the intimacy side. In the same verse where wives are instructed to respect their husbands (Eph. 5:33), husbands are to love their wives. The word for love used there for husbands towards their wives is the kind of love that God has for us (agapaō). It is huge, sacrificial and rich. In the book of Titus, women are instructed to love their husbands as well (Titus 2:4). The word used for love there is a different word. It is the kind of love we humans have for God (philandros). It is more limited, describing a friendship. I find this very interesting. Men, when was the last time you felt that your love in the marriage was to be greater, stronger and more sacrificial than your wife's? Husbands, if you want to use the Bible to describe your marriage, might I suggest that you start right here.

A pastor at one of the churches my wife and I once attended said something at a Sunday service that stuck with me. He said that commitment and discipline were not about control, but love. I like that. Growing up, I was too influenced by unhealthy power. I experienced a blend of criticism and guilt and over-control. As a result, commitment and discipline still strike fear in me and leave a strong distaste in my mouth. I see them as ways to wield power over me. But the pastor's words brought me comfort. In a more balanced environment that has a healthy blend of power and intimacy, commitment and discipline could mean love. It would place me more on the intimacy side of the equation. I needed to move further to the other side of the equation. Commitment is really showing others that they matter and that you care or love them. I like that! Self-discipline, therefore, is loving yourself. The act of self-discipline is showing yourself that you matter. You are only going to sacrifice for something that has value. When you say no to something you know to be harmful to your long-term future, you are telling yourself that you are important.

Remember, intimacy is earned. If you think about "Avatar," Jake was given intimacy into the Na'vi community due to the trust he built. The Na'vi were reluctant to bring Jake in, but he had earned it. It would have been foolish to allow him in any other way. What's more, because Jake had to earn that intimacy, he valued it. Win-win! When Jake broke the Na'vi's trust, however, he had to work to rebuild it and gain back the intimacy he had lost. Intimacy is earned, but forgiveness is given.

This idea is covered in a wonderful book I have used for years called *How to Forgive When You Don't Know How* by Bishop and Grunte. It nicely describes forgiveness as an act of love to oneself whenever someone hurts us. Forgiveness is a letting go of the pain and toxic emotions it carries. It is the job of the offended. Restored fellowship is the job of the offender. This is exactly what we are talking about in relationships with your partner. We must allow our partners to feel the loss of intimacy and work hard to reconcile themselves back to us.

Know: Forgiveness and acts of love are given. Trust and intimacy are earned.

Consider: Think about the difference between acts of love and intimacy in the life of Jesus as well as your own.

Do: Work on your intimacy boundaries this week based on the attitude and actions of others.

Chapter 5

FITTING PEOPLE INTO THE FORMULA

"If ever there is tomorrow when we're not together... there is something you must always remember. You are braver than you believe, stronger than you seem, and smarter than you think. But the most important thing is, even if we're apart. I'll always be with you." — Winnie the Pooh

I love this quote from Winnie the Pooh. Like others, the author of this favorite children's series has come across the power and intimacy formula for a happy life. Power: *braver, stronger, and smarter*. Intimacy: *I'll always be with you*. Keep an eye out for this lost formula and you will find it in the strangest places.

One of the wonderful things about these lost keys is that they are helpful at their simplest level and interesting in their greater complexity. Did you ever notice how many of the most enjoyable things in life tend to work that way? My dad took up golf in his later years. I used to laugh at the great extent to which he went to understand the game. He would sit for hours and analyze his golf swing and break it down into detail. He would study books and magazines well into the evening. Yet as a child, I just liked going out and hitting the ball. The Bible is another example. Charles Hodge once said that the Bible can be simple enough for little babes to understand or deep enough for scholars to never exhaust its riches. One could benefit from its simplest truths and its deeper complexity as well. That has certainly been the case for me.

Most of us can quickly get a sense for which side of the power-intimacy continuum on which we tend to land. By combining this with the knowledge that the more we add on one side of this equation the less we will have on the other, we have a powerful tool. This principle has had a profound impact in my personal life. I now have a goal to focus on balancing or neutralizing my life so I can thrive. Not only that, but as I change and rebalance, I am improving my relationships and thereby improving the lives of others as well. What a tremendous idea!

Without understanding this power and intimacy formula, dating can be dangerous. No matter how hard we try, we may find ourselves repeating the same unhealthy relational patterns that got us into trouble in the first place. When I first started counseling, I had a dear client named Sally. She had grown up in a codependent relationship with her mother. She hadn't been treated well and tried very hard to please her mother and win her love. Her mother had all the power. Sally came to me feeling hopeless in her inability to find someone who would be a good match for her. She liked the idea of power and intimacy that I shared with her. Then she found someone who seemed caring and loving. At first glance, it seemed like a good match, but the relationship did not survive because she realized that it was a repeat of her relationship with her mother. Only later on did she realize that this person was also self-centered and too low on intimacy.

As I was less experienced at reading people using this formula, I was misled as well. I first thought of people high in power as people avoiders. As I worked with Sally, however, I began to see there are some people who are high on power who seek intimacy but don't give it. I soon identified two styles of high-power individuals as well as two styles of high-intimacy individuals. There are high-power individuals who seek intimacy (active power) and high-power people who avoid intimacy (passive power). Likewise, there are high-intimacy individuals who seek power (active intimacy) and high-intimacy individuals who avoid power (passive intimacy).

Over the years, as I have come to better identify these four styles, I have seen loose correlations with Winnie the Pooh characters that help illustrate the differences between them. Whenever I use these styles in their Winnie the Pooh descriptors, I will be referring to them in their healthy state. It is clear to me that each of the four styles in their somewhat balanced P/I formulas (4, 5, 6 combinations) are healthy and positive. If we can keep them in a somewhat balanced formula, we can be proud of whichever of the four styles we tend to express. Jesus displayed all four styles in his earthly ministry in a positive way, and so can we. It is only when the power and intimacy imbalance is extreme (8/2, 9/1, 10/0) that these qualities can take on a more negative connotation. We must all be careful that we do not become too extreme with an imbalance that causes us heartache and unhealthy living.

High-Power People

There are two styles of high-power individuals: passive power and active power. There are people who tend to avoid people to feel powerful. This is passive power. Conversely, there are people who pursue or influence other people to feel powerful. This is active power. The first type avoids intimacy, whereas the second type tends to pursue intimacy. Let's take a look closer at each type.

Passive-power individuals: In its healthy context, these are people who know how to take care of themselves. They are good with boundaries. They make sure they do not get taken advantage of by others. In Winnie the Pooh, Rabbit fits this descriptor. Rabbit was able to take care of himself and avoid others. Passive-power individuals know that if they are going to be any good to other people, they must be good to themselves. This type of person can go it alone and create new ideas and new trends. Jesus used this style when he stole away on his own to pray. Another example is when as a youngster Jesus told his parents he must be about his Father's business and remained at the temple.

In its more extreme P/I combinations, passive power can become unhealthy. These people tend to avoid people too much. They find personal intimacy and vulnerability unattractive and their concept of power is "You don't control or hurt me." This would include people like Scrooge and the Grinch. People like this would rather avoid others since they are seen to be hurtful.

These people have very few friends and can be seen as *under-involved emotionally.*

Active-power individuals: In its healthy context, these are people who influence others. They are great leaders. They can be charismatic. In Winnie the Pooh, Tigger is an example of this. Tigger was able to influence others. Because active-power individuals are somewhat less connected to a person's feelings, they can make the tough decisions that benefit the majority at the cost of the individual. Individuals who fall into this category have little trouble with confrontation or persuasion. Jesus had no problem being confrontational with the Pharisees on many occasions. Most of us are familiar with the story of Jesus cleansing the temple and turning over the tables. When Peter tried to tell Jesus not to die on a cross, Jesus was quick to rebuke him. Jesus could also stand up on a hill and give the Sermon on the Mount to hundreds of listeners. This is active power in a positive context.

Those who are too imbalanced are not attracted to personal intimacy or vulnerability and their concept of power is "I control others." Citizen Cane and the Godfather are examples. They can be social but insensitive to the hurt they cause. They can be too focused on themselves and look at others as objects for their own gain. Another kind of active power is expressed by people who take on a parental role toward others. This concept of power is "I am responsible for others." These individuals can become behaviorally codependent. Either type of active power can be seen as *over-involved behaviorally.*

High-Intimacy People

Just as there are two styles of high power people, there are two styles of high-intimacy people: passive intimacy and active intimacy. Just as the power side has an active and passive style, so does the intimacy side. There are people who tend to avoid being powerful to be cared for or liked by others. This is passive intimacy. There are other people who pursue (emotionally) others to be cared for or liked by them. This is active intimacy.

Passive-intimacy individuals: If we first look at the positive side of this descriptor, we will find people who are easy to get along with. These individuals are non-confrontational. They can be submissive to the ideas of others. Their submission and weakness can also draw others out to become more relational as they seem safe. Winnie the Pooh is an example of this type. He relies on Christopher Robin to take care of him and help him out of his troubles. Winnie the Pooh has very few worries. Passive-intimacy people are not interested in personal power. They are strong in the area of faith and trust and are comfortable believing in the ability of others. Their concept of intimacy is "someone takes care of me." Jesus displayed this trait when he submitted to the Father and trusted in his goodness. Jesus used this role of vulnerability numerous times to draw others into a more active lifestyle. The story of the woman at the well (John 4) is a classic example of Jesus using personal need and vulnerability to change a life. Jesus, a Jew, asked a Samaritan woman for a drink of water. His expression of vulnerability to someone considered so low in the Jewish culture drew her out into a place of positive change in her life.

A more extreme unhealthy version of this might be the stereotypical blonde as we saw in Goldie Hawn on "Laugh-In" or the character of Cherrio on "Glee." Sometimes this can be the man who does nothing around the house and cannot keep a job like Al Bundy in "Married with Children." People on this side of the spectrum can be seen as *under-involved behaviorally.*

Active-intimacy individuals: In a positive vein, this is the caring, giving person. People in this category know how to be empathetic and affectionate. There is a wonderful, nurturing spirit that comes from these individuals that shows tenderness and kindness. These people can be great encouragers who have a tendency to see the glass as half full rather than half empty. Piglet is an example of this. He is a loyal friend willing to give to others. This kind of person tends to always see the good in people and will avoid giving up on them. There are many examples of this in the life of Christ. We can see this with the woman caught in adultery (John 8). Jesus was not condemning but encouraging and forgiving to her. When Mary and Martha wept at the death of their brother Lazarus, Jesus wept with them.

If active intimacy becomes too extreme, however, it can become unhealthy. We see this in people who become over-caring, people-pleasing, and enabling. They are codependent. Like high-intimacy people who display passive intimacy, they are not interested in personal power. Instead, their concept of intimacy is "I care for others who don't care so much for me." In the classic television show "All in the Family," Edith was a classic example of this. In today's world, we also see this in the show "Monk." Monk is a detective who has all kinds of obsessive-compulsive tendencies and avoids people. Natalie, his secretary, tries repeatedly to help him become more emotionally engaged. Natalie is another example of someone with active intimacy. She gives and gives to people who do not give back. Eventually it comes at too high a price—her self-respect. People with this style can be seen as *over-involved emotionally*.

In a nutshell, high-power people think the world is all about who's in control. High-intimacy people think the world is more about who cares. In the world of the Hundred Acre Wood, we have Rabbit, who has a passive-power style. He can separate from others. We have Tigger, who has an active-power style. He can influence others. On the high intimacy side, we have Pooh, who has a passive-intimacy style. He can trust others. Then we have Piglet, who has an active-intimacy style. He can care about others.

Once I type people as Winnie the Pooh characters, listeners start to place the rest of the characters into the formula. Christopher Robin seems very healthy and balanced in the middle. Kanga and Roo seem fairly healthy. The others we can guess about. I believe Beaver is a passive-power type who uses work to avoid others. Eeyore is an interesting character; I think many of us are familiar with this type of person. Eeyore is fairly balanced but he is not putting out much power or intimacy. People with depression or addictions can produce very low levels of power and intimacy. We must be careful not to try and supply both sides of the equation to them, but help them learn to develop their own.

When it comes to real people, however, it is hard to type them without a good amount of information. One test that I like to use is the TJTA or Taylor-Johnson Temperament Analysis. The nice thing about this test is that it places people in nine different personality categories. Many of these traits can help place someone in the right power and intimacy category. The TJTA types cover such characteristics as Nervous vs. Composed, Depressive vs. Light-Hearted, Active-Social vs. Quiet, Expressive-Responsive vs. Inhibited, Sympathetic vs. Indifferent, Subjective vs. Objective, Dominant vs. Submissive, Hostile vs. Tolerant, Self-disciplined vs. Impulsive. These traits are very helpful in categorizing where someone may fall on the P/I scale. Whenever I see couples who are preparing for marriage, I will give them the TJTA. Not only does it help them learn about each other, it also helps me to share this idea about power and intimacy and give a pretty good assessment of where each person can be typed. These tools can then help a couple to see the areas of their lives where work can be done.

The best way to determine what category someone falls into is to look at their characteristics as a whole. Right away, you can see that high-power people tend to be more in charge and high-intimacy people tend to be more submissive. Let's take a look at each specific category. The passive-power person can put up boundaries and be protective. Overly passive-power people like Scrooge are not going to be very sympathetic, caring, or social. The active-power person can be in charge and overcome difficulties. Overly active-power people like the Godfather can be more social but are not as caring and sympathetic. On the intimacy side, the passive-intimacy types can be easy to get along with. Overly passive-intimacy types, like the Marilyn Monroe stereotype, are less likely to be in charge of others and can tend to be less caring—they want others to care for them. Active-intimacy people can be kind, caring, and loyal. Overly active-intimacy types like Edith Bunker are going to be more sympathetic, over-caring, and codependent.

Interactive power and intimacy: All four of these traits have positive qualities in themselves if the person does not fall into the extreme range of the scale. The goal is for everyone to move toward a balanced blend (5/5) to be happier and more successful in their relationships. We will call a balanced lifestyle that is not too passive or too active "interactive." It is interactive in that it presents power and intimacy at just the right moment in just the right way. "Like apples of gold in settings of silver is a word spoken in right circumstances" (Prov. 25:11). People who are able to balance power and intimacy and use them appropriately are a reflection of the life God has designed for us and one we see in Jesus Christ. Let me encourage you to be aware of what style is easiest for you to express and what style is the most difficult for you to express. The goal of becoming more balanced would be to use your style that is the weakest more in certain situations. Along with that, it would beneficial to not use your style that is the strongest in certain situations.

In the next few chapters we will look at each of the four types in their more extreme unhealthy versions to highlight some of the drawbacks to an unbalanced lifestyle. Before we do, feel free to take the following simple test to determine your dominant type.

Circle the statements below that you find true about yourself. On the following page you will find the scoring answers to discover which Power and Intimacy type is your most dominant.

1. I'm not much of a people person and I can be just fine when I'm alone.
2. I care a lot about others and I sometimes neglect myself in the process.
3. I find myself being respected by people more than being liked.
4. I like being vulnerable and I enjoy sharing with another person how I'm feeling.
5. I like being in charge of other people.
6. I love getting together with people and can readily adapt to different social settings.
7. I like to do projects by myself and working with groups is not my preference.
8. I find myself being liked by people more than being respected.
9. I don't really like to lead groups and I prefer to do whatever the group decides.
10. I tend to be easily influenced by others.
11. Sometimes I care so much about people that I find myself getting hurt a lot.
12. I like things done right and I will tell others when their work isn't right.
13. I like it when things are already planned out for me by someone else.
14. I get exhausted when I'm around people too much and I seem to recharge when I'm alone.
15. I tend to influence others or direct others more than they do me.
16. I want to achieve and excel and it doesn't bother me if others suffer some in the process.

Find the sentences you circled below. Add up each of your circled statements for each of the categories. Your highest score is your dominant type. The scores in the last categories of Power and Intimacy will simply help confirm whether you tend to be more of a Power or more of an Intimacy person.

ACTIVE POWER (Tigger)--Total_____
I tend to influence others or direct others more than they do me. #15
I like things done right and I will tell others when their work isn't right. #12
I like being in charge of other people. #5

PASSIVE POWER (Rabbit)--Total_____
I like to do projects by myself and working with groups is not my preference. #7
I'm not much of a people person and I can be just fine when I'm alone. #1
I get exhausted when I'm around people too much and I seem to recharge when I'm alone. #14

ACTIVE INTIMACY (Pooh)--Total_____
I can care about others and sometimes I neglect myself in the process. #2
Sometimes I care so much about people that I find myself getting hurt a lot. #11
I like being vulnerable and I enjoy sharing with another person how I feel. #4

PASSIVE INTIMACY (Piglet)--Total_____
I don't really like to lead groups much and I prefer to do whatever the group decides. #9
I like it when things are already planned out for me by someone else. #13
I tend to be easily influenced by others. #10

POWER—Total_____

I want to achieve and excel and it doesn't bother me if others suffer some in the process. #16

I find myself being respected by people more than being liked. # 3

INTIMACY—Total_____

I love getting together with people and can readily adapt to different social settings. #6

I find myself being liked by people more than being respected. #8

The purpose of learning your type is to be aware of your strengths and also to work on the areas that are not as strong for you. The goal is for each of us to be able to use all of the different types in the right amount at the right time. This balance of the Power and Intimacy formula will give us the successful relationships we all long to have.

POWER -------------------- INTIMACY

ACTIVE/POWER

- Tigger
- Influential, leadership
- Dominant to others
- Over involved behaviorally
- The Godfather, Citizen Cane

PASSIVE/ POWER

- Rabbit
- Eeyore, Beaver
- Independent
- Caring for self
- Under-involved emotionally
- Scrooge, Grinch

POWER ------------------- INTIMACY

PASSIVE/INTIMACY

- Winnie the Pooh
- Trusting, dependent
- Submissive to others
- Under-involved behaviorally
- Cherrio in "Glee," Goldie Hawn in "Laugh-In"

ACTIVE/INTIMACY

- Piglet
- Expressive-responsive
- Caring for others
- Over-involved emotionally
- Edith Bunker on "All in the Family," Natalie on "Monk"

Know: There are four styles in the Power and Intimacy formula: Tigger, Rabbit, Winnie the Pooh, Piglet.

Consider: Learn which style is your strongest and which style is your weakest.

Do: Talk to your partner about your different styles and how they may possibly play off of each other. Learn to use each style in the right place at the right time.

Chapter 6

PASSIVE POWER

"I tell you Max, I don't know why I ever leave this place. I've got all the company I need right here." — The Grinch

Passive-power individuals are not comfortable with emotional closeness. Vulnerability is not their forte'. After all, relationships hurt. For this reason, boundaries are the strength of the intimacy avoider. They don't want any part of intimacy. Ebenezer Scrooge is a perfect example. So is the Grinch who stole Christmas. I love the Jim Carey version of this tale. Just like Scrooge, the Grinch was hurt and rejected. Tired of the pain, he looked for isolation to avoid it. You may know people like this. Many war veterans suffer from this syndrome as they return and deal with the effects of post-traumatic stress disorder. An article in *Vietnow* describes it this way:

> Escape became a necessity, yet it was never complete. Whenever sleep took over, there were nightmares and night sweats, causing an adrenaline rush, headaches, and nausea. Vigilance was a way of life, and family expectations were painful. Crowds and social engagements were avoided with a variety of excuses and reactions, and fights or arguments were plentiful. Weapons were on hand or nearby at all times, and there was an overwhelming need to isolate. Due to lack of concentration, confinement, and authority issues, employment was a challenge. Emotionally intimate relationships were out of the question. Any shortcut for a temporary escape was embraced, including alcohol, drugs, sex, and compulsive physical work. For some, escape meant going deep into the mountains or the woods, or taking a long ride on a motorcycle. More than 30 years later they would say, "I had no idea all of that was a normal response to combat." (Vietnow, 4/18/12)

Passive-power individuals are not social. They do not want to be with others much and have trouble sharing their feelings. They tend to be indifferent rather than sympathetic to people and their problems. How does the Grinch try to attain his power? He does it by being critical. Criticism and obsessive-compulsiveness are effective defense mechanisms. They are wonderful tools to keep others out.

Joe was a passive-power person, too. He was an airline pilot—and a perfectionist. Perfectionism works great for his job. He could, however, focus too much on how other people are incompetent and not measuring up. He saw his wife and children the same way. People were not as important as competency. I'm sure he received a real sense of empowerment by putting others down. Protection is his strong point. As an airline pilot, he finds solace in his job, which fosters his way of life. Doing the right thing is critical in his work. His lack of emotional attachment sets him up for a life of infidelity and isolation from his family as he struggles to understand love. When you look at Joe, you wonder what came first, his job or his way of life.

There are other ways passive-power individuals keep people at a distance. Besides perfectionism and a critical spirit, some use depression. Depression is a real consequence of loss. Depressed people who have gone through pain need a time out from relationships. Relationships open one up to possible pain. At the same time, depression can also make a wonderful boundary for others. The depressed person is not available emotionally and is incapable of being vulnerable. The depressed person has given up giving to others. Some people use depression as a way to control or manipulate those around them. It is very tempting to give and give to the depressed person in an effort to help them. Unfortunately, the depressed person can become a black hole. When one person is giving and the other is taking, it is a recipe for disaster. We must help depressed people start caring for themselves and others. People who are healthy can be described as being like stars with planets circling around them. Stars give warmth and light and therefore have lots of company. Does your relationship feel like a solar system or a black hole? Hopefully, it is a solar system.

Eeyore could be described as a passive-power person like Rabbit. Rabbit avoids giving intimacy by being critical. Eeyore

47

avoids intimacy by being negative. By his mood, Eeyore begs others to jump in and get involved. He does not do well nurturing himself; that's someone else's job. When dealing with depressed people like Eeyore, we must make sure that we help them be self-reliant. We must be careful not to simply make them dependent on others to provide power or intimacy. Depressed people can use depression to get others to provide power or intimacy by getting them to do things for them or pull them in emotionally. In story "The Blustery Day," Eeyore found a house for Owl. Unfortunately, it was Piglet's house. Because Eeyore is so depressed, it is difficult for anyone to stand up and confront him. Piglet, the over-caring intimacy person, of course, gives up his house. Unfortunately, this unselfish act may not be so healthy. Beaver might fall into the same category as Rabbit and Eeyore (passive-power people). While Rabbit uses criticism to keep others out and Eeyore uses depression, Beaver uses work. Workaholics do not place a high value on relationships and can use work to avoid being vulnerable.

It is interesting to see the way people try to get power in their lives. As we discussed earlier, the decree for man to be empowered came back in the garden of Eden and encompassed three different aspects. One was overcoming the environment as illustrated by Tigger. One was the role of a worker like Beaver. One was the role of a guard/protector like Rabbit. So much can be gleaned from a psychological assessment of the Hundred Acre Wood! Passive-power types like Beaver, Rabbit, and Eeyore will have to come to grips with the realization that loneliness is unbearable. Otherwise, they will endure a life of emotional emptiness. They need to come to grips with the fact that the risk of being hurt is better than the risk of being alone. As the song says, love is surely like a rose. My wife and I once rented a house that had a group of rose bushes. I was never sure how I felt about them. They were so beautiful and smelled so nice, but man those thorns hurt! The sweet smell of intimacy comes at a risk of being snagged by the thorns of rejection. For the passive-power person, becoming more vulnerable is a very difficult road. Loneliness can drive intimacy avoiders to try again, but they have so much pain that they are leery of trying to reengage. Many times, passive-power individuals believe that intimacy is not healthy.

Another metaphor that can help illustrate the intimacy/pain dilemma is one I once used with a young man whose mother had left the family. He had tremendous hurt toward his mother. The rejection and abandonment were constantly close. I told him that it is kind of like a make-believe country in which all the food comes with some curry in it. This "curry" is the vulnerability we all need in relationships to make them enjoyable and successful. I told him that it was as if he had been given super mega doses of curry when he was little and now he cannot tolerate curry at all. The problem is that in this make-believe world, all food comes with curry. If he doesn't get used to curry, he won't eat. If he won't eat, he will die. If he is to survive, he must work at slowly and safely bringing curry back into his diet. Vulnerability or intimacy is the same way. We must all risk being intimate to enjoy the rich reward relationships can bring. The intimacy avoider must slowly and safely work at bringing back vulnerability into his relationships.

One of the most important tools I've used for the passive-power person has been the power and intimacy formula. When intimacy avoiders realize that the goal of a better life is to keep some power and balance that with intimacy, they are encouraged to try. The fear of swinging like a pendulum from extreme loneliness to extreme vulnerability is taken away. Passive-power individuals can increase their intimacy and rebalance. For these people, it is important to realize that the very nature of love has a component of vulnerability to it.

There are a lot of hurting people who are afraid to give love. They desire to receive love, but they are not willing to give it. Research has pointed to the importance of giving love to have a healthy life. It has been reported that lack of love causing social isolation increases the risk of early death by up to five times. Feeling connected is also essential to good health. We may pay a price if we don't give love. Loving acts neutralize the kind of negative emotions that adversely affect immune, endocrine, and cardiovascular function. Expressing your feelings of affection can reduce cholesterol levels. A study in *Human Communication Research* found that people who wrote about their feelings of affection for significant friends, relatives, and/or romantic partners had significantly lower cholesterol levels than those who didn't.

For those people who are hurt and hesitant to reach out, it may help for them to start with very safe, small steps. I enjoy the book *The Five Love Languages* by Gary Chapman. This book describes the expression of love in five basic categories: words of affirmation, quality time, receiving gifts, acts of service, and physical touch. By using this book, passive-power people can find their favorite love language and learn what their spouse's favorite love language is as well. By simplifying the steps to showing love, passive-power individuals can learn to take small, defined steps to gradually increase intimacy.

This book was tremendously helpful for my wife and me. I found out that I like acts of service the most. I grew up with a wonderful mom who was a terrific homemaker. We always had clean clothes, a clean house, and food on the table. My mom was a doer, so that's how I interpret love. My least favorite language is touch. I grew up in Coral Gables, Florida. I was constantly dealing with sunburn, sweat, humidity, you name it. Nobody wanted to touch or be touched. My wife was the complete opposite. Her primary love language is touch. She loves back massages, to tickle my arm, and other forms of physical touch. Her mother comes over, also a wonderful woman, and she is always tickling my children's backs and asking them to tickle hers. Of course, my children would come to me and ask me to tickle them, too. Yuck! My wife's least favorite love language is acts of service. We're complete opposites. When I come home from a long day and my love bucket has been drained, I'm looking for love in my language. I'm hoping for a clean house, food on the table, and milk in the fridge. Instead, the house might be a disaster. Laundry is all over the couch, dishes are stacked up, and there is no food cooking! I have a wonderful wife, but we're all human, and days will be days. I'm frustrated and angry!

My love language hasn't been met! So I walk across the room grumbling and figure it is up to me to love myself. My wife has had a hard day. She is looking for love in her language—touch. I don't even say hello or give her a hug. I just walk across the room grumbling. So she figures she has to get the love she wants on her own as well. She comes over and says, "How about a hello and a hug?" Now I'm really bothered. Not only does she not love me in my language, but she's preventing me from loving myself! So we blow up and don't talk to each other for the rest of the night. Sound familiar? It was very helpful for us to agree to work on loving each other in the other person's language. Now I'm working to be more affectionate and she's working to do more acts of service. The intimacy avoider can find this encouraging and motivating because it makes the process of learning to give love less overwhelming. By starting with small, accessible steps, intimacy avoiders can begin to care about others to rebalance.

Alfred Lord Tennyson lived from 1809 till 1892. While attending Trinity College at Cambridge, he became friends with Arthur Hallam. Arthur Hallam was a fellow poet and close friend. He was also engaged to Lord Tennyson's sister. Before the two could marry, Arthur died of a brain hemorrhage. In a piece written in memory of his friend, Lord Tennyson penned that familiar line: "'Tis better to have loved and lost than never to have loved at all."

Know: If you learn the rules and obey the instructions, love is very rewarding.

Consider: Think of those in your life who have brought positive intimacy to you.

Do: Do an act of kindness this week. It will be worth it.

Chapter 7

ACTIVE POWER

[Kay is threatening to take the children away]

"Don't you know that I would use all of my power to prevent something like that from happening?" — Michael ("The Godfather II")

When it comes to illustrating power, "The Godfather" movies are classics. Just as Scrooge is an example of passive power, The Godfather is a classic example of active power. Michael Corleone uses people for his benefit. He does not care if he hurts people along the way as long as he gets stronger and feels safer and becomes more successful.

Active-power individuals can be very good leaders. They will make things happen and have great accomplishments. Because they can focus more on the value of success than people, they often can make the tough choices. In our examples in Winnie-the-Pooh, Tigger represents the power-dominant person who is an active-power type. How does Tigger exert his power? Through his behavior. His actions can be insensitive at times. He acts first and thinks later. In my practice, it is common to see this behavior in bipolar people. They are out to change the world. Take the example of Jim, a very competent over-achiever. When he is manic, he will take on the world and be very successful at it. Unfortunately, others get hurt in the process. Of course, Jim is self-employed. It is too difficult for him to get along with people in authority. He is the master of his own destiny. Because it is too difficult to deal with others, Jim finds ways to sabotage his success. There is no way Jim can maintain that much energy. He starts to feel overwhelmed and can have severe anger outbreaks. The stress can become too much to take. Consistency is impossible, and depression sets in. Bipolar people are so focused on achievement that they don't have time for others. Consequently, people married to bipolar spouses frequently tell me they feel like they are just holding on for the ride. When the person is in a manic stage, they are too busy achieving. When they are in the depressed stage, they are too busy being "down" to foster their relationships. In a way, the bipolar person is fluctuating between being an active-power person in the manic stage and being a passive-power person in the depressed stage.

Let's look at another Winnie the Pooh character, Owl. We could place Owl on the power side of the continuum (active power). Just as Tigger uses his behavior to affect others, Owl uses his intelligence. Sometimes power people use their own sense of intelligence and competency to positively influence others. Sometimes they use it to belittle them. Perhaps you have come across a few people like this. They are the kind who have several diplomas or licenses on their walls and tend to make you feel as if you are a lower-than-human form of life. Good ole' Oz in the Wizard of Oz is a perfect example. These people are too afraid to be vulnerable. It is much safer to be smart. Owl could be self-centered. He always saw his ideas as more important than those of others. He would go on talking and talking and was insensitive to whether others cared about what he was saying or not. These kinds of people can be the toughest to identify because they become very good at disguising their true motives. They do not really care much how their actions affect those around them. Their goal is to take from others or use them for their own gain. Other people are seen as important only for what they have to offer them.

When I was first developing the power/intimacy equation, I wondered how I might help the high power types. I would share the unhappiness that can occur when there is an imbalance. Typically, men tend to fall on the power side and women tend to fall on the intimacy side. Very often, the intimacy people are highly motivated to change and improve their life balance. They are tired of being unloved and taken advantage of and are highly motivated to put up boundaries to gain safety and respect. Meanwhile, power people are not interested in change. For several years, this stumped me. How to motivate the power person to rebalance? After all, they are not the ones being hurt. Why become more vulnerable? Many times, they are able to squeeze out love and intimacy they need.

Then I hit upon a book by Susan Forward called *Emotional Blackmail*. In it, she notes that there are three common ways that people use emotional blackmail to try to get the love they need. They are fear, obligation, and guilt (or FOG for short). People who don't offer intimacy on their own find themselves starving for it. But instead of sharing intimacy to receive intimacy, they try to force it from others. Unfortunately, what they get in return never seems to satisfy. I now use the book with my clients, telling them that there are three types of love. We can equate each of them to types of water that we get in our house.

The first type of love is no love. If there is no water in our house, we don't live long. The same it is with love. I experienced the power of "no water" when we had a water pipe valve break in our house. I thought I would save money and fix it myself. My wife and the girls were going to my mother-in-law's for the weekend and it was just my son and me. I thought this would be a fun adventure. My son still remembers the weekend in vivid detail. It was the weekend he got to pee in the backyard! We turned off the water to the house and started working on the valve. I must have gone to the hardware seven times that Saturday. I easily spent $50. Now there was no turning back. I bought a blow torch and was ready to solder the pipes together. I worked for hours but couldn't keep the pipes dry. Sunday afternoon, the rest of the family returned and there was still no water. Then I realized that no water meant no showers. No flushing toilets. No dishwasher. Help! Having a plumber come and fix the problem was some of the best money I ever spent. The second type of love is conditional love. It is like water we get from a well that hasn't been properly filtered. It keeps us alive, but it tastes and smells terrible. The third type of love is unconditional love. It is like fresh water from a mountain stream. It is fresh, clean, and pure. It tastes wonderful.

The difference between conditional and unconditional love can be visualized as me putting a gun to your head and saying you have to love me or I will kill you by the end of the week. You work really hard, but by the end of the week I'm not feeling anything. My heart doesn't really feel satisfied. My relational thirst has not been quenched. I see you working hard, but there's no sincerity. It does not feel genuine. So I figure the problem must be you. I must have to push harder on you to get the love I need. So I'll put two guns to your head next week and kill you twice over if you don't love me. You work twice as hard, but by the end of the week, I'm still not feeling it. It isn't until I put the gun down and say to you, "You can leave or you can pick this gun up and use it against me," and you say to me, "I don't want to; I want to stay here and love you." Ah! That tastes sweet! That feels like fresh water from a mountain stream! That's the kind of love that quenches. It is unconditional. It isn't conditioned on your survival or anything else. You gave me that love freely. That is what power people are missing out on when they use emotional blackmail. It sometimes helps a power person to realize that.

I had a wonderful couple come in to my office. David and Cheryl had been married for four years. David was a very hard worker. He was driven. Cheryl was from a well-to-do family. She had been able to buy whatever she wanted growing up, so David's hard-working lifestyle seemed very attractive. At first, things were great. But when the first children arrived, life got frustrating. David became critical and demanding. He was never home much. Work had become overwhelming. Finally, Cheryl had enough. She was miserable and secretly started having an affair. Soon, the couple decided to separate. After a couple of months, both had short-term relationships with other people. Neither was happy, so they decided to get back together and try one more time. That's when they came into my office. Do you know what made them unable to move forward? David had discovered that his wife had cheated on him before they separated. Of course, he had forgotten how she had tried to tell him how unhappy she was. David had used the gun of emotional blackmail most of their marriage and now he was full bore with it again. What heartbreak.

Fortunately, this story had a happy ending. David was a fast learner who liked to succeed. When I shared that he was contributing to an unhappy marriage with his conditional love, he changed dramatically. I suggested that he was a very successful businessman because he took initiative. David did not sit around blaming others. He was an overcomer! He saw that in his marriage he was the complete opposite. He was reactive instead of proactive. Part of the gun-to-head approach is creating a blame/powerless position. David was sitting around pointing the finger at his wife. Once he realized how effective he was at work by being proactive, he decided to start being proactive in his marriage, too. David stopped focusing on what his wife wasn't doing and started focusing on what he could be doing. He started to share his hurts and feelings with her.

In relationships, it is always better to be in a proactive than a reactive position. When I used to run anger management classes, the men who had been arrested for domestic violence would often use the reactive approach. I would ask them to tell me what got them arrested and into my class. They would often say that it was their wife's fault, the cop was a jerk, and the judge was mean. Oh yeah, and their boss was really rude to them and that's why they got arrested and were in my class. I couldn't help but smile. I would say, "Gee it is too bad you are in such a powerless position. You're telling me you cannot have a good day until all these other people have good days, too. That's a victim mentality!"

Active-power individuals are all about power, so telling them that they are victim-oriented is the last thing they want to hear—that they are powerless! Then I'd say, "If I were you, I'd rather say that the reason I am in the class is because I messed up. That way, I'm in control of my life. I am empowered to take some action and change my world. That seems much better to me." They loved this idea.

David is a power person: an active-power person who is overly critical. There really isn't a clear person in the Winnie-the-Pooh story who fits that picture. Rabbit sometimes fluctuates into being critical of others, so he mostly displays passive power, but when he becomes critical and judgmental, he displays active power. This brings up a good point that people can blend different parts of the power and intimacy sides of the formula, but they end up more to one side than the other. Critical and judgmental people are overly involved behaviorally with others. These people find a large part of their focus in making sure others behave a certain way. This is a huge undertaking. How can any of us really control others? Trying to do so can easily lead to anxiety, depression, and anger at the huge amount of energy required to take on such a feat. We might as well try to keep the wind from blowing!

I had another client awhile back named Bill. Unfortunately, Bill wasn't the most attractive fellow out there, but he was smart and driven. Bill might have used his smarts and driven personality to compensate for his mediocre looks. Instead, he was miserable and alone. Very quickly, it was easy to see why. Growing up, Bill watched his father and mother. Bill's father would always distance himself when he made a mistake. Bill's mother would try very hard to console and encourage her husband, but Bill's dad would reject her efforts. Now Bill was repeating the same pattern.

Bill came to my office complaining that he felt nothing in life mattered. Nothing was worth investing in. He had considered suicide at times. He was upset with himself because he felt that he had pushed a girl away whom he really liked. Bill was motivated to change, but he said he felt something blocked him from changing. I told him I would try to help him look differently at his situation and be free of his problem. I suggested that Bill look at what he was doing as prideful. Perhaps he felt too good, too competent over others. If I had felt I was not very competent, I would eagerly look for advice from others. But if I thought I was far superior, then their advice would be useless. Bill said that I may have just hit the nail on the head. He was stuck in a viscous cycle. Because he had elevated his ego so high to protect himself, it needed a lot of feeding. Bill enjoyed the boost to his ego when he rejected help and people kept trying harder to show him love. "Boy, I must be pretty important if they keep trying to pursue me with all my rejections!"

Poor Bill was stuck in the mucky water of emotional blackmail. When he began to see his dilemma, he was motivated to humble himself and find true love. Like the Wizard of Oz, Bill learned that being honest and humble is a much better life to live. The next time you look to someone else to solve all your problems, just make sure you pay attention to the man in the mirror.

I'm starting with the man in
  the mirror
I'm asking him to change
  his ways
And no message could have
  been any clearer
If you wanna make the world
  a better place

  (if you wanna make the
world a better place)
Take a look at yourself, and
  then make a change

  — Michael Jackson, "Man in the Mirror"

There is another type of person who can fall into the active-power role as well. It is the codependent caretaker. These are usually people who control others, not so much to use them as to reassure themselves that they are good people. Sometimes they are in the role simply out of survival. Other times they picked up this role early in life when they were given too much responsibility at too young an age. These people can be said to be "parentified." Usually their partners have dropped the ball in many areas of their lives. Caretakers take on a parent role and their partners move into a child role. This relationship does not support the deep, rich intimacy that comes when partners relate to another as adults.

These active-power types are over-responsible behaviorally. They are codependent by trying to turn power into intimacy. By decreasing their power and increasing their vulnerability to rebalance, the active-power types can find the happiness they're looking for in life.

Know: Unconditional love can only be given. It cannot be taken.

Consider: Think of people in your life who have used emotional blackmail.

Do: Show unconditional love this week by refusing any emotional blackmail invitations.

Chapter 8

ACTIVE INTIMACY

"When you please others in hopes of being accepted, you lose your self-worth in the process." — Dave Pelzer

Dave Pelzer is well known for his book *A Child Called 'It.'* In the book, Dave recounts a life of abuse from an alcoholic mother and an uninvolved father. The book describes horrific abuse and Dave's plight to find someone who cared for him. Pelzer faced the difficulty of eating scraps and tolerating physical abuse in an effort to be loved by his mother. I like his statement that we can lose our own self-worth as we seek to be accepted. Extreme intimacy-dominant individuals who use active intimacy also face the loss of their own self-worth for the sake of acceptance from others. Active-intimacy types tend to provide too much intimacy to people who haven't earned it. They are over-responsible emotionally. As people begin to pour out intimacy to those who haven't earned it, they are subtly telling the other person that they themselves do not have much self-worth. They convey the message that it does not cost anything to have their fellowship or intimacy.

Sometimes the messages we give to others are not healthy ones. While we may think of vulnerability as showing love, *over-*vulnerability does not really love a person in a healthy way. Ironically, it actually hurts them. How? People who receive intimacy without paying the price of giving it can become callous and self-centered. If we truly love someone, we have to do things that help them become better people, even if our actions are met with resistance. Many times, active-intimacy people are afraid to do the difficult things that might cause conflict.

Whenever I work with clients in this role, I sometimes purposely tell them they are being somewhat self-centered. In a way, they can be too self-centered because they're trying to protect themselves by being over-caring.

These clients do not want to think of themselves as selfish, and telling them that they are has just enough Tabasco sauce on it to motivate them to change! What do I mean by Tabasco sauce? I enjoy a donut now and then, but put Tabasco sauce on it and I am not going to touch it. In fact, the thought of a donut with Tabasco sauce is downright repulsive. Now we're talking about aversion therapy. I've lost my appetite! Sometimes when our ideas have a little Tabasco sauce poured on them, it helps us to change. I always explain this ahead of time so my clients don't take me as insulting. The intimacy person may try to please the power person by showing love and affection and thereby obtain safety through their partner's protection. The result is an overdependence on another. As I always tell my clients, you cannot marry what you're missing! If active-intimacy individuals will look to themselves and do the things that increase their own power, they will truly be empowered.

The extreme active-intimacy types can become overly focused on helping others to the neglect of themselves. This is a trap that can be common in the helping professions. A nice benefit of my job is that I'm more like a golf instructor than a physician. I had a physician in my office for counseling once. He is a terrific guy. He really cares about his patients, but it was getting the best of him. He told me he would stay up at night trying to figure out why his patients were ill. He was becoming overstressed and losing out to burnout. He told me his patients were depending on him. They had nowhere else to go. If they had stomach pain, they were looking to him and the medical field to save them. My job is quite different. I'm giving my clients tools to help them help themselves. If you want to help someone you love, be a golf instructor! Don't play golf for them. Teach them to golf!

How could I help this doctor who felt such a burden? I had to help him change his viewpoint. He was motivated by over-caring. I had to sour the milk on his position. I had to put Tabasco sauce on the donuts. I suggested that he was making himself too important to the process. Maybe he was even being a little self-centered. That's some awfully hot Tabasco sauce! I encouraged him to be part of the solution, not make himself the only solution. Jesus was a big proponent of each of us being responsible only for ourselves. Think about the rich young ruler who wanted to follow Jesus. Jesus told him to sell all he had and come follow him. The rich young ruler turned and walked away. Did you notice that Jesus let him? Jesus didn't chase after him and yell, "Wait, wait, you're making a big mistake!" Neither did Jesus say, "Gosh, I really messed that up. I probably said the wrong thing. This is my fault. I feel terrible." Jesus allowed the young ruler to make his own decisions. He let many turn away from him with his confusing parables.

When we take responsibility only for ourselves, we actually open ourselves up to be more loving. I've had a number of ladies see that in couples counseling. In two cases, their husbands were sharing something that bothered them and both of these ladies' initial responses were very similar. The first thing they said was, "Gee, I didn't think I was doing something wrong. I feel frustrated and confused. Could someone tell me what I should have done differently?" Do you see what happened? Their husbands did not feel heard or cared for. Right away, the wives focused on themselves and looked to see what they did wrong. They didn't have time to focus on others and show empathy and validation. One of the ladies called this over-responsibility the "dragon." She spent most of her attention on what she didn't do and had little to focus on loving others. By not being overly responsible for others, we are free to show love and kindness. Paul talks about that in his letter to the Romans when he says, "Rejoice with those who rejoice, and weep with those who weep" (Rom. 12:15). We are called to allow others to have their feelings and honor those feelings, not take responsibility for them.

When I work with clients who are trying to change their thinking about over-giving, I give them tools I like to call a few p's. These are words that start with the letter "p." I find that most people focus on not doing the same thing again. "Don't eat that donut, don't eat that donut." So guess what we do? We eat the donut. To illustrate, I'll often tell clients, "Don't think of pink elephants flying in the sky. *Don't* think of pink elephants flying in the sky." What do they do? Yep, flying pink elephants are all they can think about! So "p" number one is, give yourself *permission* to think about anything. That way, you take the energy away from the very thing you are trying to avoid. In other words, you are no longer feeding the monster. The next "p" is *prefer* to think about something else. Now you are focusing your energy on something positive.

Thirdly, *poison* the old thoughts you are trying get rid of. That's where the Tabasco sauce comes into play. If you find yourself drifting back to thoughts you're trying to break, poison them. I had a couple come into my office because the husband had been unfaithful several times in their marriage. The husband was contrite, but he wasn't sure he wouldn't do it again. When I asked him about his thinking, it is no wonder he felt that way. He had painted a picture of his temptation that was unrealistic. As I listened to his thinking, it became clear that he needed to poison his thoughts. If a man thinks that the woman he sees at the gym is going to be the best thing since pea soup, no wonder he's going to pursue her. I tell him to try poisoning those fantasies. Instead of seeing some romantic, exciting rendezvous, I suggested that he try picturing a woman with a crazy boyfriend with a knife or a woman knocking on his front door with his children standing behind him, crying. I told him to imagine some woman who has every sexually transmitted disease possible. That's what I call poisoning an image!

"P" number four is *powerless*. Sometimes it helps us to avoid troubling thoughts by making them powerless. I had a lady come into my office who was troubled by very negative thoughts. She would worry about her boss yelling at her. I suggested she picture her boss holding a bouquet of flowers surrounded by cartoon animals. She couldn't help but smile. The idea seemed to take the sting away. In her mind, her boss had become softer and less threatening.

One last "p" is making something *positive*. When I was in grad school, the big word of the day was to "reframe" a person's world to help them cope and grow. I had a teenaged girl who was very angry because her parents had gotten divorced and her grandmother had passed away in the same year. As the girl talked about her grandmother, it was obvious her grandmother was special. I asked what her grandmother would want for her. She said she would want her to grow up to be successful and caring. I told this young girl that these things in her life could be a blessing. She probably has more wisdom and maturity than other girls her age because of all she has gone through. She could actually be more successful and more caring because of them. She could use these experiences to give back to her grandmother the wish she had for her. What a wonderful way to honor someone who meant that much to her! Her world had been reframed. She was able to take a very negative year and look at it in more positive terms.

Despite having some of these tools, active-intimacy types have a hard time with not over-giving when they have been treated poorly. Many times they feel that providing intimacy will make things better in every situation. I have had more than one lady in my office with the same complaint. One is a wonderful Christian woman whom any man would be thankful to have as a spouse. She comes into my office and complains that she is being treated very poorly by her husband. On the outside, he looks very competent and can even be active in church. But at home, he is emotionally and verbally abusive.

I remember the power and control wheel from the Duluth model in my days of leading anger management classes. These wheels highlight the different areas that can be used by people to exert their power. Men who are too controlling can use economic abuse, isolation, children, male privilege, and intimidation to name a few. (Male privilege can mean it's okay for men to have free time or be unfaithful, but for women it is not.) These men fit the wheel. They exert an unhealthy type of power with no thought of its effect on intimacy. They are power people who have not figured out the formula to happiness. When their wives go to pastors or friends and ask for help and guidance, many times the advice is to stay in the situation and continue to love their husbands and eventually they will come around. Sounds enabling, doesn't it? Sometimes the advisors will quote Bible verses such as 1 Peter 3.1: "In the same way, you wives, be submissive to your own husbands so that even if any of them are disobedient to the word, they may be won without a word by the behavior of their wives."

Let's take a look at that advice through the power and intimacy lens. The verse says, "Be submissive," but we've earlier discovered that submission is not the same thing as intimacy. My advice has been to be submissive and respectful; wives can even show their husbands acts of love. Acts of love are an expression of intimacy but are not intimacy itself. Sex is also an expression of intimacy, but it is not intimacy. I would, however, support a wife refusing to have sex with her husband if she is being mistreated as it would be the best thing to do not only for her own self-worth but also for her spouse. I am a strong believer in biblical ethics. By that I mean if you face a conflict in biblical commands, I believe God supports the choice of the greater good. In the book of Joshua, Rahab the harlot lied to save the lives of the spies and was blessed by God. The act of a wife refusing to have sex with an abusive husband helps him see that his actions matter. There are consequences! Regardless if one chooses to avoid sexual relations, turn off the intimacy! That is biblical!

As I pointed out earlier, the Bible uses the word fellowship. I don't know about you, but if I don't pay the water bill, the water doesn't keep coming to my house. There are consequences to our actions.

I may say that these women did as I suggested, and it was effective! They also felt more empowerment. They were rebalancing themselves, and it was having a positive effect on their marriages. That is another great thing about this formula. If I am rebalancing, it will—in turn—rebalance others.

There are two ways to increase power for those who tend to be too high on the intimacy side of the continuum. One is to become more confrontational. The other is to withdraw emotionally. For intimacy people, it can be much easier to withdraw emotionally than to be confrontational. Confronting the power person usually ends in volatility, and the intimacy person fails in the end. Power people, by their very nature, are not good with intimacy. There aren't usually too many places a power person knows where to turn for real care and love. In other words, if you are an intimacy person and you are dealing with a power person, you have something very valuable. You have a commodity that is very important to them. If you shut down intimacy and are determined to keep it off until there is true reconciliation and change of behavior, you will see clear improvement!

Because active-intimacy people tend to give too much intimacy, they can withdraw intimacy to rebalance. I have seen several women who have saved their marriages by making this simple change. In the power and control wheel, the wheel becomes renamed. Instead of the power and control wheel, it becomes the equality wheel. It still touches on the same areas, but those areas are now seen in a much healthier way. If you look at some of the new areas in the redefined wheel, you can pick out the balance of power and intimacy. Some of the areas cover things like trust, honesty, respect, and economic partnership. Here again, we find the power and intimacy formula in another helpful tool.

Know: Focusing too much on what we may have done wrong can block our ability to care for others.

Consider: The difference between acts of love and acts of intimacy.

Do: Work on giving your emotional intimacy only to someone who has earned it.

Chapter 9

PASSIVE INTIMACY

Brittany: "I was pretty sure Dr. Pepper was a Dentist." —
"Glee"

Passive-intimacy individuals seem so cute it is hard to get frustrated with them. They have that little child presence that we all enjoy. The problem is that they are adults with a little child mentality. We have seen this kind of person from generation to generation. We have seen it in the Marilyn Monroe types to the Goldie Hawn types in "Laugh-In" to the Brittany role in "Glee."

One of my favorite shows has been "Pawn Stars." What fun to learn a little about history with the added bonus of negotiations! On that show, we see the male version of the passive-intimacy person in Chumlee. Chumlee plays the part of the stupid, silly friend who always has the good one-liners. He is a passive-intimacy type. Years ago, we saw that role in comedy duos like Martin and Lewis, Abbott and Costello, and even way back to Laurel and Hardy. All had a power avoider in their skits. Such people are lot of fun, but how can you respect someone like that? My father-in-law used to love Laurel and Hardy. We would sit together and I would watch him laugh and laugh. His favorite skit was the one in which Stanley drank a whole cup of soda instead of sharing half with his friend Oliver. Oliver asked why he didn't leave half the soda in the cup for him. Stanley started crying and replied, "I couldn't! My half was on the bottom!"

Passive-intimacy people do not love other people very well. They tend to be more focused on getting others to love them. In a way, these people can be unknowingly selfish, wanting to be loved but not willing to pay the price of loving others. This is the classic "dumb blonde" we have seen over the years. When it comes to people in that role, we don't expect much from them. They have a sort of free pass on life. How could someone like that be expected to succeed or care much about others? Our attraction to them is that they make us laugh and help us feel empowered. How could we not feel competent and successful in comparison to someone who thinks Dr. Pepper is a dentist?

Passive-intimacy types like Winnie the Pooh use being cute or child-like as a way to get others to take care of them and love them. As a therapist, I would take note of this when someone would come into the office displaying some of these qualities. Many times, these people had been overly cared for as children. They had been trained to be dependent on someone else. For others, the attraction to such people is that if they get into a relationship, they would have all the power. That can be an attractive trap for some people. When we see someone who is helpless, it is tempting to come in and take care of them. That would seemingly increase my power. Unfortunately, their helplessness is a black hole that never ends. The person who takes the bait feels very powerful at first but soon begins to feel very power*less* since nothing they do is enough to help. It is a never-ending pit of lost energy.

Again, you cannot marry what you're missing. Claire was like that. She would drink too much alcohol then do something self-destructive. She was giving a clear invitation to family and friends to help. Of course, the help they gave was not enough. Then through guilt and obligation, she would trap her victims. Those victims were stuck trying over and over to find ways to help her. I would encourage Claire to get out of the victim role (more Tabasco). Who likes to think of themselves that way? Claire's powerlessness was not giving her the care and love she wanted. In fact, her powerlessness was actually pushing people away. She was feeling very alone and unloved. This was a dangerous place in which Claire might be tempted to use this unloved feeling to further trap others. It was important for Claire to see that her actions were pushing people away. She has to learn that her power and intimacy equation is off balance. Claire has an attractive quality of high intimacy with a repelling quality of low power. Claire ends up being very much like the donut in the window you wish you never had.

Other people use sex appeal as a way to draw people in. What a nice, easy shortcut around the work necessary to be responsible for themselves. But what do they do when the sex appeal wears off? Once again, the person is left in a difficult place. I had another wonderful client, Carol, who grew up being very attractive. As a teenager, she got a lot of what she wanted through her looks. When she got older, she kept trying to stay young. She had been through one marriage and another was on its way out. She had always picked a man who was on the power side of the equation. The first marriage was with an active-power type. He was abusive and unfaithful. She hoped her second marriage would be different. She married a passive-power type. It hadn't faired much better. Now in her fifties, she was trying hard to look young and pretty. I suggested that she become more balanced with power and intimacy in her life. She started looking to herself to find happiness. She had her breasts enlargements removed. She started dressing more her age and looking more natural. Her idea of the perfect man started to change. She started looking for someone who was also more balanced. After her marriage dissolved, she found a much different man than she had ever had before. This was a man who had a lot more intimacy in his life. She had a balanced relationship and a happy life.

Some people use humor as a way to draw people to them. We see this in the role of the jokester or class clown. Larry had grown up with a critical father. His mother gave him a lot of attention, especially when he was funny and cute. Larry avoided confrontation because his dad could be mean and intimidating. So as Larry grew up, he used his ability to make people laugh as a way to get by. However, while people were laughing, they didn't respect him. Sure, they liked him because he was funny. But nobody really wanted to be his friend. Larry was pursuing power people, hoping that they would like him. Unfortunately, it didn't work—just like the person who uses sex appeal. What is he going to do when he's not funny? Larry started to work on his boundaries. He started to give opposing opinions. Larry was working at rebalancing his life to find happiness.

This is exactly what George McFly had to do in "Back to the Future." George had a nemesis named Biff who bullied him, and George put up with it. Finally, George stood up to Biff and his entire future changed. He put up boundaries and found the happiness he was looking for. Power avoiders tend to be too powerless, but they can increase their power to rebalance. When it comes to making changes, it is always easier to start with new relationships than relationships that have become ingrained over the years. For example, the relationship with your parents is probably the last relationship to try to change! It is much easier to start with someone with whom you have not yet developed a pattern in the first place.

If someone wanted to get out of the power-avoiding role, I would encourage them to start simple. Start having an opinion. Start having a preference. I love the section in Stephen Covey's book *Seven Secrets of Highly Effective People* about being proactive: using "I" statements and getting rid of the phrase, "I don't know." These are all helpful ways to rebalance and get out of the power-avoider role. Another way for power avoiders to rebalance is to become more competent. Competent people are powerful because they are knowledgeable and able to do things on their own. I had a woman in my office who used both the withdrawal technique of the active-intimacy type and the competency technique of the passive-intimacy type to radically improve her marriage.

Many times, we give off messages that we don't realize. The phrase that has been used is *meta messages*. Meta comes from the Greek meaning "after" or "beyond." It carries with it the idea that something else is received besides the original message. In my counseling sessions, I describe it this way. I turn my chair away, and with my back to the client, I tell them I really care about them. My mouth says one thing, but my body says another. Which message is stronger? In 1971, a study by Albert Mehrabian suggested that 55 percent of communication is body language and 38 percent is tone of voice. I don't think much has changed in human nature, do you? This only leaves 7% of our message being in the words we use. We must be willing to look at ourselves and become more aware of the messages we are sending to others.

The one problem with the role of the high-intimacy person is that the power side of the equation has some important qualities we all need. It brings respect from others and freedom of choice, which are critical to our emotional survival. High-intimacy people believe they can find happiness in life by living in a way that avoids conflict and avoids taking responsibility for their own lives, but that choice does not take into account the importance of those qualities from the other side of the P/I equation. In an effort to be cared for, such people lose other important qualities, such as their self-worth. In the end, they find life frustratingly unhappy.

This is really the case with all four types we have covered. Each of these types is choosing a pattern that they believe to help them be successful. However, they do not choose a balanced meal for life. In a way, all of it can be summed up in that each of us must promote these qualities in our lives and not look for ways to take them from others. Passive-intimacy individuals can increase their power to rebalance their lives and find joy and happiness.

Know: Allowing others to be responsible for your life is not the best intimacy.

Consider: In what ways do you seek intimacy?

Do: Express healthy power by avoiding laying blame or making excuses.

Chapter 10

POWER, INTIMACY, AND CONFLICT

"Knowledge is power." — Francis Bacon

Francis Bacon was someone who believed that learning was important and empowering. Most of us are familiar with his scientific method, which he established back in the 1600s. Francis Bacon was so gripped by the importance of learning and growing that he ended up dying of pneumonia resulting from one of his experiments. Healthy people are those who are growing and working on healing their wounds in an effort to become healthier.

The act of healing can be both empowering and relational. When one becomes aware of his wounds, he now has the *power* to act. He also has the ability to communicate his needs with others in a better way, increasing his *intimacy*. Back in chapter one, we talked about thinking about power and intimacy as you would soil in your backyard. When the soil is balanced and not too acidic or too alkaline, it allows plants to grow and thrive. This is evidence that the soil is healthy—plants are growing and flowers are blooming.

One helpful tool I have come across to help our "soil" thrive is a book that describes conflict as an imaginary house with three floors (*Spouse Abuse*, 1984). These three floors help us to build better intimacy with others. The three floors describe the focus of our relational conflict. I tweaked their names so that each floor has one word to describe it.

The first floor is attacking a *problem.* That might be me coming home late from work and wanting some milk. I go to the fridge and there is none. I say to my wife, "Hey, Kimberly, would you mind going to the store and getting me some milk?" She says, "Gee, it is nine at night and I'm in my pajamas, I'll go tomorrow, but I really don't want to go tonight." Bummer! I really wanted that milk tonight, so I say, "I guess I'll go and be back in ten minutes. Bye." That couple stayed on the first floor. They looked at a problem and found a solution.

Of course, that doesn't always happen. We often go to the second floor and attack the *person*! I might say, "What have you been doing all day that there's no milk in the fridge? Are you kidding me?" I've just gone after her character. I'm no longer trying to solve a problem. I'm suggesting my wife is lazy, irresponsible, and self-centered. She will then fire back with, "You were on the computer for three hours last night. If you wanted your milk, you could have figured it out last night!" She's attacking my character as well. She's saying the same thing to me. I'm lazy, self-centered, and irresponsible. This couple will continue with the same round and round argument: "You're so selfish!" "No, *you're* the selfish one!" Clearly, they are on the second floor.

If the pattern continues, they will ultimately get to the third floor and start attacking the *partnership*. "I don't even know why we're married!" "Well, there's the door buddy. Why don't you leave?" "Okay, I'm out of here!" Boy, I know this pattern all too well. My wife and I used to argue a lot. We would go through that whole house in under five minutes. We needed to stay in the first floor!

When we look at healthy relationships, we will talk about ways to stay on that first floor. But one thing I wanted to explore was something I noticed early on in my work with couples. It might be great to stay in that first floor, but while it is great that we don't escalate the situation, sometimes it feels as if we are still dealing with the same problems over and over. My wife noticed that with me. I found I actually have "milk in the fridge" problem. My wife said to me once, "You know, John, you really seem to get upset when you come home and we are out of milk." Ouch! She was right! I found that conflict house has a basement! Things from our past become problems on today's first floor! We have wounds that need healing. I like to call them *core wounds* or *core issues*. These are things from our past that we are still healing from. I tell clients that it is as if someone has been tapping on my arm with a pen for fifteen hours. At first it doesn't hurt so much. But after awhile, it gets to a point of intense pain. If someone new walked into the room and picked up a pen and started tapping all over me, I would be fine until they hit on that one spot. Ouch! We all have that one spot—in fact, most likely several spots. Core wounds.

Core wounds can come in one of two ways. They are either something that was negative in my life and has left a wound or something that was positive in my life but is now gone. Both can leave painful wounds.

The milk in the fridge was the latter for me. When I started to think of people in my life who would have contributed to the "milk in the fridge" wound, I thought of my mother first. Bingo. She was a positive in my life. Being an Irish Catholic mom, she was a servant. She loved me by being a homemaker. Clean house, clean sheets, good meals, food in the cupboard, and milk in the fridge. I came back to Kimberly and said, "I figured it out! I was trying to make you my mommy!" There was a wound of losing my mom and I was hoping that she would cover it up so I wouldn't have to face it. That was powerful! I had put someone else in charge of my healing and didn't even realize it. Once I owned my wounds, I was free to look for ways to heal them. I was no longer a victim to others. Here I was, wounded and waiting till 9 p.m. at night and hoping someone would help me, and not even knowing where the emotional bleeding was coming from. Now with this new awareness, I was on the road to healing.

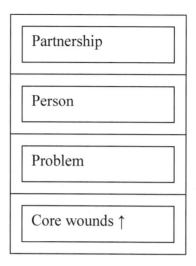

Once I began dealing with my emotional wounds, I found that my approach to others changed as well. I began sharing with my wife how important milk in the fridge is to me. This went over far better than the "you're so selfish" line. I shared where this wound came from and why milk in the fridge is so important. What do you know? Kimberly said she would try to be sensitive to that and try to make sure we had milk in the fridge. It is kind of like sharing you have a sunburn on your back, and once those close to you know about the sunburn, it makes them want to get out the ointment to help you feel better. It also makes them want to be careful not to hit you on your back. Boy, this is working well. This process has added power by awareness and intimacy by changing my approach to others! This is somewhat similar to Michael White's Narrative Therapy, which tends to externalize or objectify problems. The benefit is that by making our problems an object (or in this case, a core issue), it helps the client gain power. The problem is the problem, not the person as the Narrative therapist would report. Of course, my wife may let me down sometimes and not always have milk in the fridge, but my healing is my responsibility, not hers. That feels good to me. I get a healthy shot of both power and intimacy in the process!

By the way, if you look at my wound, it was due to a loss of power and intimacy both. Wounds can be one or the other or both. This one was both. My mom loved me by bringing *power* of physical security (food, shelter, and so on) to me along with emotional *intimacy*. That says something for the relationship that combines both healthy power and intimacy!

One thing that I have found that really helps in the healing process is to value ourselves in regard to healing those wounds. It always tickles me how much we humans neglect our emotional wounds but focus on our physical ones. I guess that makes sense given that we cannot see our emotional bleeding, so sometimes it is harder to value it.

Here's where I'm going with this. One day I was coming home late and had a hard day. I was looking forward to that nice glass of milk to get the love I needed—a boost of power (physiological needs) and intimacy (memory of a loving mom). But I also loved to tuck one of my daughters into bed at night and she always fell asleep very early (she still does). In my new awareness, I called home and asked about the milk in the fridge as well as the status of our daughter. My wife told me that we were out of milk and she was sorry that she didn't get a chance to get any. Secondly, my daughter was waiting for me, but she was close to falling asleep.

Great. Now what do I do? I often ask my clients what they would have done. You know what most of them say? Most say I should have tucked my daughter in and then gone to get my milk. You know what would have happened if I had done that? I would have felt so tired and unloved that I would have lost my cool, yelled at my children, and looked like a schmuck. Ever been there? So I tried something different. I decided to get my milk first. By the time I got home, my daughter had fallen asleep, which was a sad thing. But I sat at the table and drank my milk. You know what? I had a dramatic healing.

It took me awhile to figure out what had happened, but now I get it. I had been neglecting my wounds. If I put this in terms of physical healing, it becomes much easier to understand. Let's say we are going to your favorite restaurant but you have stomach flu. Are you coming with us? Of course not. You have severe sunburn and we're going to your favorite beach. Are you coming with us? Of course not. You broke your leg and we are going to play your favorite sport, basketball. Are you coming with us? Definitely not. Why is it so easy for us to tend to our physical sounds, but emotionally we rarely see it so clearly? What better way to heal than to pick your healing over other things you value? What an emotional boost it is when you tell yourself that you are more important than other important things in your life.

Don't get me wrong. I'm not saying my daughter is not valuable. But when you look at the value of not putting her to bed *one night* compared to healing a deep emotional wound that helps me be a better father in the long run — it was well worth it. With my healing, I am better able to be a good father, husband, and human being. If you are going to pour your cup out to others, you must have something in it. If you're on an airplane and the air masks come down, who do you put the mask on first? You or your children? It better be you. Otherwise, you won't be in a position to help your children because you'll be passed out from lack of oxygen. Healthy people are self-valuing people. This actually helps those around them as well. Most of us think in competitive terms, but it comes with the American culture, I guess. Stephen Covey hit on this idea with his *7 Habits of Highly Effective People*. Habit #4 was "Think win/win."

A person who has a healthy balance of power and intimacy is not only growing but is optimistic and caring. The optimism comes mostly from the power and the caring comes mostly from having intimacy. What a beautiful combination. Who wouldn't be attracted to someone who is growing and achieving as well as kind and empathetic? When someone is optimistic, it is because they believe in success. The power person believes things will happen. Because they also have an equal amount of intimacy, they also believe that people are important and that people will contribute to that success. An optimistic person believes in the ability to accomplish and change one's environment. On the intimacy side, along with the optimism comes a sense of helping others. The intimacy side of a person sees the worth in other people. Because people are important to the intimacy person, they take time to help others and show people they are valuable. Doesn't this sound like the kind of partner we all would want in life?

Diane was someone who could really use that message. She was frustrated that her in-laws did not like her as much as she would have hoped. She kept bugging her husband to stand up for her and defend her. That is a nice thing to do for your wife, but she was trying to force him by nagging. How do you think the in-laws would perceive the situation? They might think less of her because they would assume she was forcing him to do it. She was not displaying power (self-worth) or intimacy (direct communication). If she would talk directly with her in-laws instead, they might be impressed with her display of power and intimacy. This is, of course, the instruction of Matthew 18. If we have an issue with someone, the Bible encourages us to go first directly to that person in private. Secondly, she kept nudging her husband to explain to his parents that it was him who was resistant to spending time with them, not her. After she realized her focus was negative, she also realized why her husband wasn't cooperating. When she turned around the idea and asked him simply to praise her without any negatives added, he was a lot more willing to be supportive. People with a balance of power and intimacy have a growing bucket and are less inclined to need to find fault in others to boost their own self-worth. The balanced power and intimacy person is growing, optimistic, and caring.

The apostle Paul touches on the importance of power and intimacy when he prays that "He [God] would grant you, according to the riches of His glory, to be strengthened with power through His Spirit in the inner man, so that Christ may dwell in your hearts through faith; and that you, being rooted and grounded in love, may be able to comprehend with all the saints what is the breadth and length and height and depth, and to know the love of Christ which surpasses knowledge, that you may be filled up to all the fullness of God. Now to Him who is able to do far more abundantly beyond all that we ask or think, according to the power that works within us" (Eph. 3:16-20). This section is a wonderful encouragement for the reader to see the importance of relational intimacy and empowerment! Paul not only focuses on the power of God in our lives, but he also talks about the love of God in the context of community. There is a power that works within *us*!

I had a young man in my office that really saw the value of this in his situation with his parents. Dominic had shared with me that his parents had come to him when they got a call from the school counselor. The counselor had told them that Dominic had flunked his science class and was running out of opportunity to make up the class. When his parents came to him, he got defensive and didn't talk. They, of course, got upset at his seeming lack of concern. He got more defensive and angry and started yelling and screaming. When he was in my office, he admitted he just felt threatened. I told him one of the best answers to feeling emotionally threatened is to be caring (intimacy) and wanting to help solve the other person's problem (power). It is not a good feeling for any of us to feel that spotlight of fear and guilt with another person. What better way to get off the hot seat than to turn the attention to the other person in a caring way? As the other person shares his or her frustration and I continue to show attention and concern, it eases my feelings of being threatened. After initially caring, I can move the direction of the discussion to finding solutions. This is the first floor of our conflict house!

As Dominic and I talked, we agreed it would do a lot if he went back to his parents and shared that he responded that way because he felt threatened. He did not want to come across that he didn't care. Now he was being intimate by sharing from his basement of the conflict house and he was ready to move up into the first floor and talk about solutions! This was a wonderful combination of intimacy and power that was sure to go far in his personal success.

The wonderful thing about this formula is the simplicity of its solution. It is very easy for anyone to remember power and intimacy. Many teenagers I have worked with have been able to quickly grab hold of this and begin to apply it to their lives for the rest of their lives! The Grinch finally laid hold of this balance by the end of the movie when he saw all those presents going over the mountain ledge,. "Oh, no, the sleigh, the presents, they'll be destroyed, and I care! What is the deal?"

Know: All of us have core wounds that are either negative experiences in our lives or positive ones that have been taken away.

Consider: Think of the things in your life that get you quickly upset. They're probably core wounds.

Do: See if you can label your core wounds and share them with those you trust.

Chapter 11

POWER, INTIMACY, AND SELF-WORTH

"Power is of two kinds. One is obtained by the fear of punishment and the other by acts of love. Power based on love is a thousand times more effective and permanent than the one derived from fear of punishment." — Mohandas Gandhi

Mohandis Gandhi cared about others but was not afraid of doing things that others did not like. That is self-worth. Gandhi had a full bucket of power and intimacy both. He could love himself and love others. Because he truly loved others, he did not look out for his well-being only. This is exactly what Paul encouraged in his letter to the Philippians: "Do not merely look out for your own personal interests, but also for the interests of others" (Phil. 2:4).

It is interesting that Paul makes the point for us to "not merely look out for [our] own personal interests." There is an underlying expectation here that we will take care of ourselves. It is nice to know that we are allowed to look out for our own personal interests. There is nothing wrong with being responsible for and taking care of ourselves. Eight times in the Bible it states, "love your neighbor," and every time it includes "as yourself." We have to be doing a pretty good job of loving ourselves if we are to love others as well. This is the essence of the power/intimacy formula. The power side is the act of loving ourselves, while the intimacy side is the act of loving others.

In this chapter, we will cover nine keys to self-worth that will help change your world. I recently shared with a client how self-worth is the key to healthy living. I went on to explain, as I will cover in the addictions chapter, that I believe the building blocks of self-worth are power and intimacy. My client replied, "You probably have lots of books on self-worth. Could you recommend one?" I stopped and thought, "Nothing comes to mind." Now I realize there must be a lot of books on self-worth, but it did hit me that there aren't enough.

This concept of self-worth or self-regard is huge to living a healthy life. After all my years of counseling, it is still the core element of therapy. There have been several therapists who have supported this idea. One of my favorites is Carl Rogers. Carl Rogers was born in the early 1900s and went on to be one of the most influential psychologists of the twentieth century. His father was a civil engineer and his mother was a strong Pentecostal Christian. Carl Rogers was one of the founders of the humanistic approach to psychology. At one point, he termed his approach "client-centered." There has been some backlash that his focus on the importance of the client promotes relativism in which there is no absolute but only what the client perceives. However, one of the things I appreciate about Carl Rogers is his focus on the importance of supporting the value of the individual. With his client-centered approach, there was a renewed emphasis on individual empowerment and competency. I remember some of the videos of Carl Rogers at work, and it seemed as if he just repeated back to the client what the client was telling him. Yet there was power in his approach. His term of giving "positive regard" helped people to be real to their own self or "congruent." To me this seemed a lot like having love and acceptance. As clients feel that love and acceptance, they feel more confident in both areas of power and intimacy.

The beauty of the power and intimacy formula is that the balance of these two things brings us a sense of self-worth. As we talked about in the previous chapter, the building blocks of a full emotional love bucket come down to power and intimacy. The power side allows us to keep our boundaries. The intimacy side allows us to be connected to others.

Let's look at the nine self-worth concepts.

Self-worth Concept #1: Make your own life the most valuable to you. Jesus did! One of the big questions I like to ask clients is, "When Jesus was here on the earth, whose life was the most important to him?" I hear a variety of answers. Many people say, "Others." What I like to say to them is, "His own life!" Think about that. In Matthew 4, Jesus refuses the devil's temptation because he knows his life is the most important! If someone told him he needed to do a miracle or go to Jerusalem and he didn't think it was the right thing to do, he didn't do it! Peter told him not to die on a cross and Jesus replied, "Get behind me, Satan!" Wow! Here is the person we would say is the most loving person who ever lived also valuing his life number one! I don't know about you, but I could sit a long time watching the sunset and think about that one. They don't conflict! You can have both!

I just had another client who recently told me that he couldn't even consider the idea that Jesus could value himself number one and still so love others. I told him that makes the loving all the more meaningful. Jesus gave something he considered extremely valuable—himself! When the Israelites were instructed to slay a lamb at Passover so the Angel of Death would not come to their doorstep, do you know what kind of a lamb it was? It was one without blemish! One that had value makes the sacrifice that much more meaningful.

This is why self-worth is such a key component to healthy living. When I think about someone lacking either power or intimacy, I imagine them to be struggling with self-worth. Much of the time when we are dealing with depression or anxiety, you can bet there is a lack of power or intimacy. When someone has a lot of power but not much intimacy, I would not expect them to be anxious necessarily, but probably more depressed. When someone has a lot of intimacy but no power, I suspect they would be more anxious. Scrooge was likely not anxious; he had all he wanted. His security and safety needs were met. But he was alone. It is very depressing to be alone. Life can be miserable. I love the quote from Mother Theresa about loneliness: "When Christ said: 'I was hungry and you fed me,' he didn't mean only the hunger for bread and for food; he also meant the hunger to be loved. Jesus himself experienced this loneliness. He came amongst his own and his own received him not, and it hurt him then and it has kept on hurting him. The same hunger, the same loneliness, the same having no one to be accepted by and to be loved and wanted by. Every human being in that case resembles Christ in his loneliness; and that is the hardest part, that's real hunger."

The person with very little power but lots of intimacy can be anxious, too. That person is like George McFly. That was an anxious fellow. Concerns about safety and well-being would cause most of us to be anxious. It is interesting that in my practice I am seeing anxiety on the rise. The way the economy has been going, many people are stressed that they may lose their jobs or their homes. People who are able to increase both power and intimacy are filling their own buckets of self-worth and are helping to prevent the destructive effects of anxiety and depression.

Self-worth Concept #2: Being angry at others can make others more important than yourself! When I used to do anger management classes, I would constantly use self-worth as a critical tool for helping my clients live better lives. When people would come into my class, they were often defensive, believing that as the therapist I would just add more shame and guilt to their own lists. It always surprised them when I would say that they were not taking good enough care of themselves and needed to think more of themselves! That had to be the last thing they were expecting.

I would tell them when they were angry with someone, they were giving away all their power to that person because that that person was now in control of their thoughts and feelings and sometimes behaviors. That's not valuing yourself very much! What is more important, I would ask them, fixing the guy who wronged you or protecting your own future? If someone cuts you off on the freeway, why would you try to fix his wrong and

84

go after him—possibly setting yourself up to be shot or go to jail? There is not much self-worth there.

Self-worth Concept #3: When you are hurt by others, don't become the bad guy! Another self-worth tool I use with anger management issues is also connected to power and intimacy. The very common terms of "passive," "aggressive," and "assertive" easily fall into the power and intimacy formula as well. The aggressive person has too much power at the cost of intimacy. The passive person has too much intimacy at the cost of power. The assertive person has a nice blend of both.

For example, if you tapped my arm for fifteen hours, it would really start to hurt. If I got so sick of it that I picked up a brick and threw it at you (aggressive), which one of us would go to jail? Me. How did I end up being the bad guy when you've been tapping my arm for fifteen hours? In a way, I took the monkey off your back and put it on my own. I don't know about you, but I've got enough of my own monkeys without putting yours on my back as well. Except for survival (throw every brick you need to throw), every time we choose to be aggressive, we become the bad guy. That doesn't work for me. I hope it doesn't work for you. We wouldn't be valuing ourselves much with that choice.

Another possibility is that you tap my arm for fifteen hours and I just leave. But the pain is now killing me. So I stop at the bar on the way home and get drunk. That seems to have stopped the pain, but I start doing this all the time. I come home late. I get a DUI. I lose my driver's license. I lose my job. Guess who the bad guy is again? Me. The passive response doesn't work either. Suddenly, I'm the one with a drinking problem. All this bad stuff is happening to me, and you—the one who has been tapping on my arm—don't have any problems. All the addictions are a passive attempt to deal with hurt in my life.

So what's left? Being assertive. What if I caught the tapping early and asked, "Would you mind stopping? That bothers me." I think some of the time, the other person would say, "Fine, sorry." That's a great start. I'm not going to jail and I don't need to go to the bar. I'm going home and playing with my children. I have

85

cultivated power and intimacy in my life. But I know sometimes the answer is, "Go jump in the lake!" I like to look at it as a tennis match of ownership. By my assertive response, I put the tennis ball back over the net where it belonged—in your court. Instead of owning it, you just shot it back over the fence at me. Now I am again faced with the same three choices I had at the beginning. I can respond to that with an aggressive, passive, or assertive response. Many people might say, "Well, I tried to be nice, so here comes the brick," or, "I tried to do the right thing, where's the bar?" But those choices are no better than they were the first time . . . or will be the fifth time or the tenth time. We have two healthy choices at that point. We can keep playing tennis with the person or stop and find someone else. That decision would be based on how valuable that relationship is to us. If it is someone I've been friends with since I was five, I'll play tennis with them for a long time. I will be up nights trying to figure a way to fix our differences. If it is someone I just met or don't even know, I'm done playing tennis. It would seem awfully unhealthy for me to blow off someone who means a lot to me as well as to invest so much of myself in someone who means nothing to me.

Self-worth Concept #4: Emotional health affects physical health. The person with anger is not valuing himself in another way as well. One of my favorite books on the topic of anger is *Anger Kills* by Redford and Redford. For that book, they did a study of people who scored high on a hostility test. They found that people who scored high had a higher rate of heart and cancer disease. In other words, anger can shorten a person's life! Now if we have high self-worth, we are going to be careful where we want to shorten our lives. Many times I've thought, is this the place where I want to shorten my life? It is amazing how many places aren't worth shortening my life for!

Self-worth Concept #5: Viewing others as less powerful than you can be healthy! Many times, when we are emotionally wounded it is because we have perceived a loss of power or intimacy. One helpful trick is a simple reframing of our world. If you were someone who loved to garden and a three-year-old from across the street walked into your backyard and told you your garden was stupid, it might hurt a little but not much. After all, it is a three-year-old. But now let's suppose the person you value the most in the whole world comes and says the same thing — that your garden is stupid. You would be devastated. I would, too. Notice that the same thing was said by two different people and your response to each was entirely different. One was not such a big deal. The other was overwhelming. The only difference was the value you gave to the words! That is powerful!

If you think everybody is more important than you are, you are going to be hurt a lot by their words. But if you think you are more important than others, their words will not do much damage to you. If we see others as hurting, weak human beings who are frail and often make mistakes (a lot like ourselves), then our bucket of self-worth will not empty as quickly. I always tell my clients that it would be nice to be able to have them tell me I stink as a counselor. If they said I'm the worst counselor they've ever known, it would only take a little teaspoon out of my bucket of self-worth.

I have a physician friend who has been a real inspiration to me. He is the epitome of my idea of power and intimacy. He is very successful in his business, yet he still has plenty of time for his family and friends. He is very sacrificial and gives freely of his time. I remember how many of his clients would just rave about him. But as the health care industry changed, he couldn't spend as much time with each client. Some of them came to me and said that they were a little disappointed by his lack of attention. One day I came in to his office for a check-up and I felt obligated to share some of their thoughts with him. I remember how impressed I was with his reaction. He simply said that it was too bad that he has had to make some changes as the industry has changed. I was impressed. There was no, "Oh no what am I going to do? The world is coming to an end!" This might have been the response of the overly intimate person. Nor was there any, "Well, they can all go jump off a cliff for all I care!" This would have been the response of the overly powerful person. There was a nice full bucket of power and intimacy that kept the response to a minimal healthy focus. While dying on the cross, Jesus was able to pray, "Father, forgive them; for they do not know what they are doing" (Luke 23:24). He was also able to display that attitude to those who were following him. "Seeing the people, He felt compassion for them, because they were distressed and dispirited like sheep without a shepherd" (Matt. 9:36).

Self-worth Concept #6: Worrying is next to useless. Worrying is all future oriented. That means all the worrying you did about past events is over. Did it help you? No? It does not help when I do it, either. Think of how much you worried about in the last couple of years that has now come and gone. We all worry about so many things. Every month we worry about bills and car problems and you name it. It manages to get taken care of somehow. Let me encourage you that you will get through most of the stuff you worry about. Take a second to think of all your past worries that have come and gone and watch your confidence grow. One of my clients came to me dealing with anxiety. Things in his life were very intimidating. Life can bring some very overwhelming feelings. I admitted that my own life has had a lot of stress and anxiety for the last few years, but I'm not anxious at all about last June's bills getting paid or any of the many things last year I stressed out about. Then it hit me! I'm still here. All of that stress is useless to me now, which meant it was pretty useless back then! Think of how many things you didn't need to be anxious about last year because you seem to be fairly okay now. *How much of what you worried about in the past is not affecting you today?* A ton! That is pretty powerful! Sometimes we're more powerful than we realize! As we are able to see ourselves with more power or more intimacy, we will see ourselves as having more self-worth.

Self-worth Concept #7: You are more than you realize. I find that many times my clients have a limited view of themselves. The decisions they make reflect the low value they place on themselves. As an example, when I was younger, the decisions I made were simply based on John the young man. Now I have grown. I am John the man. I am not only John the man, but I am also John the father, John the husband, John the churchgoer, and John the counselor. When I make a decision, I need to consider all these different hats and how it will affect them. This is exactly what I want you to consider in your life. You are more than you realize. Make choices based on all the different hats you wear!

Self-worth Concept #8: Protect the intangible (invisible) things as much as the tangible (visible) ones! I find that clients often focus more on the tangible things than the intangible things. Many times, they will get very upset if someone cuts in front of them or takes something without asking for it. Even people can be seen as objects. But how much do they value peace and harmony or trust? If someone was married and developed a trusting relationship over twenty faithful years, that's intangible but of infinite value. Nobody could buy that at any cost. You cannot order it on the Internet. You cannot buy it with one million dollars. Likewise, if you value yourself, you will put a high price on the intangible things in your life, too. Value the invisible. I love what Paul says to the Corinthians, "for the things which are seen are temporal, but the things which are not seen are eternal" (2 Cor. 4:18).

Self-worth Concept #9: Fixing you fixes your world! This self-worth approach in the balanced power and intimacy life is infectious. We all feed off other people's behaviors. When I first started working with clients on this idea, I would use a simple tool to help them see the power of a healthy life. I would take the client's folder and ask them to pretend it was an imaginary boundary between us. I would hold the folder between us and move it close to them. I would tell them this boundary meant that I was in charge of my life and their life. Then I would move the folder close to me and tell them that this meant they were in charge of their life and mine. Moving the folder into the middle meant that each of us was equally in charge of our own selves. I then went on to say that they had just made a decision to keep the folder in the healthy middle with all people. This means that someone might come up to them and push their folder toward them and say, "I'm going to tell you what to do and say." Of

89

course, they would then want to push it out to the middle in order to stay healthy. Someone else would come up to them and pull the folder away and say, "You are going to take care of me and tell me what to do and say." Again, they would move the folder back to the middle and refuse to let their healthy boundary to be moved.

Then I would tell them something really exciting. Even though they are just focusing on taking care of themselves, guess what? They have just pushed or pulled everyone else into a healthy boundary as well! That wasn't their focus or their concern. It was simply a byproduct of healthy living. If your boundary is healthy, you will draw everyone you come in contact with into a healthy boundary, too.

This is the beauty of the power and intimacy formula. If you are a 5/5, you are drawing me into a healthy 5/5 formula as a byproduct of healthy living. It is contagious! There is a passage in the book of Matthew in the Sermon on the Mount in which Jesus says we are not to take the speck out of our brother's eye when we have a log in our own eyes. It never usually goes over very well. Jesus then follows with the message that we are not to "cast our pearls before swine." It is interesting that he follows up that verse with a message about not judging someone. What Jesus is saying is that usually when you point out faults to another, your efforts will rarely be received positively. You may have some great pearl of insight, but we must be careful not to share it with someone who is not open to receiving it.

I'm so glad the story of Jesus cleansing the temple is found in the Bible, too. Here again is another message about the importance of valuing yourself. I know we have all heard about turning the other cheek and giving a man a coat when he asks for a shirt, but when I read the story of Jesus getting angry at the money changers for making a buck at the cost of sincere worshipers, I never see him turn the other cheek. He didn't offer to help carry all the money home or clean up the mess left on the ground. He threw tables over! When I ask clients what was going on in the story, they tell me the temple was not being treated with respect. Okay, where is the temple today? (1 Cor. 6:19).

According to the Bible, believers are the temple of God. So it is okay to value the temple of God. Nowhere else do we see Jesus so angry and fired up as in that passage.

The wonderful thing about the P/I formula is that we are positively affecting others when we work on changing ourselves. There is comfort in knowing many times we can help fix another by fixing ourselves.

I had a client come into my office and share a thought from one of Jon Courson's messages on Luke 9:23: "And He was saying to them all, 'If anyone wishes to come after Me, he must deny himself, and take up his cross daily and follow Me.'" Jon said that the idea of denying yourself is not like saying "no" to chocolate (so it doesn't have anything to do with lack of self-care). It is more of acknowledging that we cannot follow him in our own power. We need God's power. That obviously entails power in our own lives. John also said that the idea of taking up Jesus' cross is not so much taking on some solitary burden like trying to break a habit. It is more an act of restoring people to God. It is a redemptive work. The cross is about relationships! That is intimacy. Following Jesus is living a life that replicates his life. That means valuing ourselves and our mission. All of that means living a life of power and intimacy.

Know: Self-worth actually helps your relationships improve.

Consider: Think about your own measure of self-worth and whether you allow yourself to be worthwhile.

Do: Do an act of self-worth but not an act of selfishness.

Chapter 12

POWER, INTIMACY, AND RELATIONAL TOOLS

"Love cannot be forced, love cannot be coaxed and teased. It comes out of heaven, unasked and unsought." — Pearl S. Buck

Pearl S. Buck was an interesting lady. She spent most of her life as a missionary to China in the early 1900s. She wrote many short stories and novels and won the Pulitzer Prize. She was also the first woman to win the Nobel peace prize in literature. She had her share of hardships, including a child with retardation, a hysterectomy early in life, and an unhappy first marriage of eighteen years. One wonders if all these experiences didn't help her stumble upon a wonderful concept about love. The best love is the kind that is freely given. Love that is not conditional upon anything else is the sweetest tasting of all. With my clients, I talk with them about that. It goes back to making sure I don't blackmail my partner. I want to look for that win/win solution. I want my wife to love me because she chooses to out of free will. Otherwise, the love I get becomes watered down. I realize that the best kind of relationship is the one in which both partners have a balanced amount of power and intimacy. I want to do anything that will support that balance in me as well as in the other person. One of the things that will help foster this is the way I talk to my partner. These are very simple things, but they are effective tools to help keep a relationship balanced.

1. Avoid questions. The use of questions is not very helpful. Think about questions for a second. Questions are taking without giving. That puts the asker in an overly powerful position. "Where were you?" "Who were you with?" "What did they say?" "What did you say?" "Why did you say that?" The asker wants intimacy but isn't giving any out. When I mention this to my clients, I say, "Let's suppose you ask me, 'Where were you last night?' Whoa! I'm a closed book. I don't know where you're going with that question. I feel defensive." Then I suggest that they turn that around. "What if you said, 'We were at the mall last night and we think we may have seen you with your daughter and were just wondering what you were up to.'" Boy, that's a lot better. Now I feel comfortable. "Yes we were looking for some shoes and then we were going to go look at sweaters." What made the difference? You were vulnerable with me. I was vulnerable with you. Most of us have had talks with our children that went something like this: "How was your day?" "Fine." "What did you do?" "Nothing." "Who did you talk to?" "Nobody." Not much intimacy going on there. Both people are at a standstill. Statements are better than questions. Some statements are better than others.

2. "I" statements are better than "you" statements. "You" statements can seem controlling or attacking. "You need to" is the kiss of death. I had a couple that worked on that forever. Ken and Jill had a pretty good relationship, but Ken felt that Jill could be too controlling. He didn't feel the power side of the equation that we all need in our relationships. Jill would constantly say things like, "You need to pick up your clothes and then you need to turn off the light. Then you need to go down and say goodnight to the children." All he could think is, "You need to jump out the window!" When Jill changed that to, "I would like" or "I would appreciate it if," it made a world of difference. People who use "I' in their vocabulary reflect self-worth. They feel comfortable with their thoughts and feelings. They don't mind sharing themselves with others. They give out the message that they are valuable and their feelings are important.

3. "I feel" is a very good opening for sharing with another person. In the field of communication, most of us are familiar with the three levels of intimacy. I describe it as looking at a cross-section of the earth. First you have the surface of the earth. These are superficial things like facts. The sky is blue. We live in a one-story house. Next are layers of soil. Those are our beliefs. Just as there is a lot of room between the surface and the core, there is a lot of room between facts and beliefs. Beliefs have some vulnerability. Beliefs are things like, "The president is doing a good job." Or, "Democracy is the best way to live." Third, you have the core of the Earth. These are our feelings. Feelings are the most vulnerable. Feelings bring about the most intimacy.

Feelings are things like, "I feel frustrated," "I feel hurt," "I feel disregarded," "I feel scared."

I have had couples come into my office who talk mostly on the surface. This is frustrating. Typically, it goes something like this: "So what brings you into my office?" Husband: "Well, we were supposed to meet at Starbucks at 4 PM." Wife: "No, it was 4:30 PM." Husband: "No, it was 4:00 PM." Wife: "No, remember your mother was going to meet us afterward at 5:00 PM." Husband: "No, we were supposed to go meet *her*." Ughhhhhh! All that communication stuck on the surface. It is like eating empty calories. There is nothing nourishing in any of it. I share the idea of the three levels of vulnerability. Then I begin to work with them to learn to communicate with each other in a more meaningful way. Sometimes that includes the very common tool of active listening. In that exercise, someone holds an object in their hands and only the person holding the object can talk. The job of the other person is to repeat back what he or she heard. Now we have people focusing on what is being said, not on what they are going to say next. I will ask them to add into their work a "finish the sentence" exercise. Something like, "and it sounds like you're feeling [fill in the blank]." Now we are into feelings!

4. Use the triangle approach. A very simple tool I have given couples is the image of a triangle. I tell them to put themselves at the top of the triangle. *The first leg of the triangle is what I want.* To help them get unlocked from this battle, I tell them that they must then try to put themselves into the other person's corner. *This is the second leg of the triangle, what you want.* By learning about the other person's position, we have just accomplished two things. First we are gathering more information to help come to a solution that will meet everyone's needs. Second we are showing the other person we care about them. The language is filled with active listening "*you*" statements. "Tell me what *you* like." "It sounds like *you* want to . . ." This is taking time to validate another person. Validation is such a crucial element for healthy relationships. Many times, the argument isn't so much what we're talking about as simply that one person doesn't feel valued and cared about. If you want to go somewhere for dinner and I want to go somewhere else, I might fight tooth and nail about my choice, but it may have little to do with where we are eating and more about the fact that I don't feel validated.

When I was early in my marriage, we had three young children. My wife had gone to visit her family for the weekend. I thought I would take the time to put lights under the eaves in our front yard so our children could run around at night. Now, I'm not a very good handyman. It took a lot of work. I drilled the wrong holes and hit my thumb with a hammer. I also got the wrong kind of lights. The lights were more like spotlights so the front yard ended up looking like Stalag 17. Anyway, when my wife got home, I rushed up to her as she was getting the cranky children out of the car (never a good idea) and asked what she thought about the lights. She said, "You're not going to keep that cord around the front window, are you?" Ouch. Being the newly licensed therapist, I thought I would try out my new tools. I told her that her statement had hurt my feelings. She said, "Well, what do you want me to do? Lie? It doesn't look good." Somehow, this wasn't going so well. I thought, "Hell could freeze over before I fix that cord. She's going to have to climb up that rickety ladder and hold onto those loose tiles on the roof and work on that cord herself!" Not the most loving thoughts. I tried to view my situation more along her line of thinking. I also waited for her to settle the children down. Another good idea! I said, "What if you worked hard all Thanksgiving to cook us a meal and I took one bite of it and said, "This stinks! It tastes terrible!" She got the idea. It also probably helped that she had time to gather herself with the children. She said, "I'm sorry, you did a great job. Thanks." You know what I did next? I went out and fixed the cord. Not only did I fix the cord, but I did it with a big smile on my face! My hurt wasn't about the cord. It was wanting to feel validated. So the next time you get into an argument, you might want to try validating the other person. It can save a lot of heartache. Healthy relationships take time to validate one another.

The last leg of the triangle is what we want. The last leg is filled with "we" statements. "Are there any ideas *we* haven't thought of yet?" Is there a compromise *we* could agree on? That leg takes real initiative and leadership. This is the leg that seems the toughest for people to achieve. It is about focusing on solutions and inviting teamwork to achieve those goals. "Blessed are the peacemakers, for they shall be called sons of God" (Matt. 5:9).

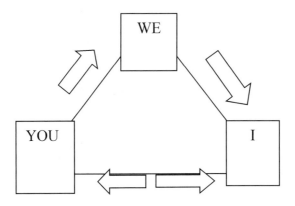

5. Add the "I.C.U.R. Upset" steps to work through the problem.

Sometimes I use an acronym to help me work through a problem with someone. The acronym I use is ICUR—the "ICUR upset" approach.

I. The "I" stands for <u>identifying</u> the problem. That's the beginning in which each person shares his or her opinions or feelings. It is important to try to share this positively rather than negatively. Think about these two phrases: "You aren't showing me any attention" and "I like it when you show me attention." One sounds condemning. The other sounds positive. The first approach could easily start an argument whereas the second might lead to positive discussion. Notice that the focus is to <u>identify the problem, not your solution to the problem.</u> Sharing the problem you are trying to solve with another is so much better for constructive and healthy communication. For example, my wife was going to see our son in Texas and said she wanted to take the laptop. That's a solution to a problem she is trying to solve. Well, the laptop has a lot of important stuff on it and I don't want it flying to Texas! Bingo, argument. However, if she would have said that she needed to get online to order tickets for our son to fly back home, that would have avoided an argument and I could have helped at finding a workable solution for everyone. So, share the problem first, and then share your idea for a solution.

C. The "C" stands for <u>caring</u> for the person and <u>clarifying</u> the problem. This is where we take the time to listen and understand another's point of view. It is making sure the problem is also accurately identified. For the listener, it is important to start by focusing on <u>identifying the hurt feelings.</u> <u>Caring</u> comes before <u>clarifying</u>. A person might say, "Sounds like your feeling...." That way the person is seen as more important than the problem and not the other way around.

U. The "U" stands for <u>unifying</u>. As we take time to listen and understand, we not only get the clarification we need, but we also <u>validate</u> the other person. We can find some truth or acknowledgement in their hurt. We might respond with a "Yeah, that is an area I need work on." Now we are becoming unified as a team and looking to come to a solution together.

R. Finally, the "R" stands for <u>rectifying</u> the problem. When we rectify a problem, we decide on a solution that is agreeable to both sides. That may be in the form of a compromise or a win/win solution. If someone is responsible for wrong-doing, taking individual ownership of it is very healing. One of the best ways to rectify a conflict, or to bring closure to it, is for both sides to find something that they did wrong and to take responsibility for it. If somebody apologizes, that is not the time to add more fuel to the fire but to respond back with an apology. Rectifying is future oriented. I cannot tell you how many clients of mine have spent way too much time arguing about the past and not moving forward into a better future.

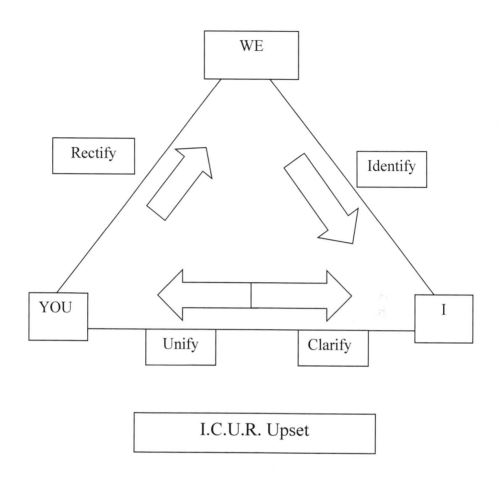

6. Appreciate compromise. This is a wonderful tool that healthy relationships employ. Many people don't like the idea of compromise, but if you look at compromise in the formula of power and intimacy, it makes complete sense. Compromise is a way of having enough power to value yourself and enough intimacy to value your partner. When my wife and I were having our fourth child, I got a taste of the importance of compromise. My wife wanted the expected girl to be called Sydney Rose Lucas. For her, Sydney was like the city in Australia where our friends live. Rose was like the beautiful flower. To me, Sydney was a big tall girl who punched me in the nose in fifth grade. Rose? To me, Rose is like that old lady in the movie "Titanic." I couldn't do it.

What I didn't realize is that my preference was being driven by a name thing we had going on that I hadn't noticed before. Our first child was Lauren. Our second child was Jordan. Then we had Madison (again, with some arguing). Each of our children had a name that ended with "N." So I thought it would be cool to have our next child keep the tradition going. Since I was half Irish, I thought maybe something like Shannon or Sharon. My wife didn't want any part of it. We worked hard at figuring a name out. We went through every baby book. We learned what each of us liked and didn't like. Still, we couldn't find a resolution. Finally, we did the David Letterman top ten. We listed our ten favorites. Lo and behold, our third choice was the same name: Allison. Now the name didn't really do a whole lot for either one of us, but it was something we both could live with. So we went with Allison.

At that point, I got really angry. I got angry at my wife for not giving me what I wanted. I got angry at God for putting me into this stupid predicament. When that girl came, I was going to be angry at her every time I had to call her Allison! Life was starting to look miserable! Then the good Lord gave me an idea. How many people have given up the name of a child for someone else? Not many. Not that many people have someone who is that valuable in their lives. I do! I'm a lucky fellow. Now I'm whistling a happy tune. I realized that whenever you give something important away for the sake of someone else, you are affirming to yourself that you have someone important in your life! Now life has changed! I told my daughter this story and she feels very important. God has taught dad something special through her life. My world looks a lot more positive now. I don't feel so resistant to compromise and giving. It continues to affirm that I have important people around me.

7. Relate adult to adult. When I was in grad school, the teachers took time to go over the different fields of psychotherapy. One was Transactional Analysis by Eric Berne. This one fits into the power and intimacy formula well. He was the person who defined our relationships in terms of transactions between different roles: the role of the parent, the child, and the adult. Many times, we can take on the role of the parent or the child with ourselves or with others. I might become a little child and irresponsibly go eat several doughnuts. My wife might take on the role of the parent and say, "You don't need those donuts." But the healthy relationship is one in which people relate to each other as adults. I remember how my professor woke up the class by giving the reason for this: "Nobody wants to have sexual intimacy with their father or daughter or mother or son." That really hit home.

It is important that each of us sees our partner as an adult. Any other role is unattractive. This is exactly what the power and intimacy formula suggests. The parent role has too much power and the child role has too much intimacy. It is only the adult role in which we have a balance of the two. I had a teacher who helped me with my counseling studies. Boy, she could take on the parent role. I would ask her a question and she would say, "Now John, I've told you this before. It is very simple. If you just read page three again." Very parental.

I have noticed that when someone is in the parent role, it is tempting for the other person to take on the child role. The same is true with power and intimacy. When someone takes on too much power, it is tempting to fill the void with too much intimacy. When someone takes on the child role, it is tempting to take on the parent role. When someone provides too much intimacy, it is tempting to bring too much power. Here is the nice thing about both of these ideas. If someone takes on the adult role (or the balanced power and intimacy role), it is tempting to take on the healthy adult role and the healthy balanced role. That is powerful. When we respond to people in a healthy way, they are tempted to respond to us in a healthy way back. The healthy relationship is one in which both people are working to meet their own needs. Each person is balanced and generating both power and intimacy. There is less stress on the relationship, less demand on each other. Now the relationship has more give to it and less take. Both people are also influencing the other to stay balanced by keeping themselves balanced. What a great picture of healthiness.

8. Be willing to take "time outs." One of the things that healthy couples are good at is taking time-outs. A time-out is a reflection of the power and intimacy formula. First it is an honor to the element of power in a person's life. It is an acknowledgement that each of us is in charge of our own life and must respect the responsibility of managing our own feelings. Each one of us is in charge of our own feelings and must wait patiently until both people are in a healthy place emotionally to work out a mutual problem. Second it is an honor to intimacy because both people are not looking only to their own problems but caring about the well-being of the other. As Paul wrote in the letter to the Philippians, "Do not merely look out for your own personal interests, but also for the interests of others" (Phil. 2:4). I love that verse because of the blend of power and intimacy suggested in its instruction. The verse says it is okay to look out for your own interests (power) as well as look out for the interests of others (intimacy).

When I suggest the time-out policy to my clients, I try to present it in a new way that adds a little tasty flavor to an old idea. What we are saying is, "You are important to me. Our relationship is very valuable to me. Life's problems are lower down on the value scale. When we begin to argue, if we don't watch it, the argument will become more important than our relationship. I don't want that to happen. So when I call a time-out, what I am saying is that I love you and our relationship is more important than the argument." That's a good thing. Now we have a good message.

Many times, conflict is the result of miscommunication. People say things in the heat of battle, and we react poorly. Things are said like, "I'm out of here!" *I'm out of here?* What does that mean? Does that mean you're divorcing me? Does that mean you're moving to Milwaukee? Or does that simply mean I don't matter to you? Now we have a phrase—"time out"—that lets me know something positive in the heat of battle. To me, it is like calling a play in the huddle in football. The play is called while things are calm so that when the ball is hiked and things get crazy, I have a plan of attack. Could you imagine football players hiking the ball and then trying to call a play? That would be crazy!

Let's take a look at some of the suggested guidelines of the time-out policy. First, make it a maximum of 24 hours. What that means is that somewhere within the next 24 hours, I promise to come back and finish talking about the problem. Why 24 hours? Sometimes it can take that much time to calm down, but it is not so long that it becomes forgotten. Sometimes my clients will say that the Bible says we should not go to bed with things unresolved. Usually what they are referring to is Ephesians 4:26: "Be angry and do not sin; do not let the sun go down on your anger." *Do not let the sun go down* is not the same thing as staying up all night until your disagreement is settled. In fact, that is actually the opposite of the verse's instruction. The verse is an encouragement for us to work on letting *go* of anger. We must learn how to manage our feelings on our own and not feel that it is up to others to sooth our emotional upheavals.

Sometimes there is no resolution to an argument. It would be nice to think that if we could only let go of our anger, things would always get fixed. But it doesn't always work that way. Throughout my years, the good Lord has chosen to leave some things "unfixed." I imagine you can think of things in your life that God has chosen to leave unfixed as well. There is an important point here that, by letting go of our agendas and the feeling that we are entitled to have things fixed all the time, we are allowing our character to be fashioned and matured. To emphasize the importance of doing away with anger, Paul goes on a few sentences later to say, "Let all bitterness and wrath and anger and clamor and slander be put away from you, along with all malice. Be kind to one another, tender-hearted, forgiving each other, just as God in Christ also has forgiven you" (Eph. 4:31, 32).

9. Minimize conflict. It has to be acknowledged that conflict, even healthy conflict, takes its toll on a relationship. One of my favorite verses in the book of Proverbs states, "The beginning of strife is like letting out water. So abandon the quarrel before it breaks out" (Prov. 17:14). Many times, conflict gets out of hand

and causes more destruction than it needs to—much as a small leak in the dam can destroy an entire town.

When it comes to visualizing the effects of conflict, one of the images I share with my clients is of two neighbors who live next door to each other. Let's say in house number one, the couple argues the first five minutes of the day and then settles the argument and the rest of the day goes fine. In house number two, they get along the first five minutes of the day and then argue for the rest of the day. They don't like each other and never settle their quarrel. If each of these couples repeats the same pattern every day of the year, that means in house number one, they don't like each other for one day out of the year (five minutes times 365 days equals 30 hours or a little over one day) and the rest of the year they love each other. Their neighbors are just the opposite. They like each other for one day and the rest of the year they cannot stand each other. Year after year like that and you have two couples going in very different directions. That is based on just one area—conflict resolution.

Know: "The anger of man does not achieve the righteousness of God" (James 1:20).

Consider: The ways you may have been destructive with relationships in the past.

Do: Choose one of the tools in this chapter you like. Make a commitment to use one this week.

Chapter 13

CLASSIC RELATIONAL COMBINATIONS

"Me and Jenny goes together like peas and carrots." —
Forrest Gump

In the movie "Forrest Gump," Jenny and Forrest seemed to fit each other's styles. Jenny is the passive-power individual who has been hurt a lot and tends to avoid intimacy. Forrest is the active-intimacy person who is willing to supply all she needs. Most often, passive-power types are men and active-intimacy individuals are women. Yet sometimes the roles are reversed. That is the case in this movie. Certain combinations of relational types seem to fit better than others even though they can sometimes be unhealthy.

Let's look at some of the most classic relational combinations.

Active-intimacy people and passive-power people: This is one of the most common relationship dynamics. We see it in the movies. We see it in life. It is a common theme that surrounds us. It is very familiar.

Active-intimacy individuals are the over-givers. They are codependent. They work really well with passive-power people like Scrooge. The key component in this relationship is the *intimacy factor*. Passive-power people who are intimacy avoiders do not show much love and care to others. They are not very relational. What better person to match with than the overly intimate person? One of my favorite television shows is "Monk." This show reflects this relational dynamic very well. Monk is the classic passive-power person and his helper Natalie is the active-intimacy person.

Carol came into my office hurt and exhausted. She had tried everything to improve her marriage. The man she had married showed her no affection and didn't communicate his feelings. She had tried all kinds of things to help improve the relationship. She had told me that when she was younger she had to take on the parent role. She had to give and care for her siblings since her parents weren't doing a good job of it. From her early years, she had become an emotional caretaker. Now she was taking on this role in her marriage. Carol left notes for her husband. She encouraged him to go to counseling with her. Nothing seemed to work. Her husband came for a few sessions and then stopped, saying he had nothing to talk about. Carol said everything seemed to be about her husband. He hardly ever took time to think about her. Carol would go to counseling, then go home and share what we had talked about, but he seemed only half-interested.

This is a very typical relationship. If I've seen one, I've seen fifty. What is interesting is that I look at these women and they are awesome. I think to myself that anybody would be lucky to be married to any one of them. I told Carol that there is a solution to this problem, but it is up to her. I also told her it was going to be hard for her to do. Carol broke down crying, telling me, "I'm exhausted! I don't think I can do any more!' I told her, "This is what you have to do—nothing." I told her that this was going to be difficult, but I believed she could do it.

Carol had been providing the water of intimacy to a household that hadn't been paying the bill. It was time to turn off the water. I encouraged her not to listen to her husband much, avoid interaction with him, and stop trying to please him. Stop trying to fix him. If Carol could turn the intimacy water off, this would put him in a position either to change or leave. Nobody can live very long in a house without water. I also told her that it is important to communicate why the water was off when she got a chance. It is kind of like the water company sending us notice to let us know what we need to do to get the water back on. By communicating only what needs to be changed, it keeps Carol in the right and does not allow her husband to twist things to avoid personal responsibility. In response, Carol's husband will try to engage her with arguments or excuses or blame. Sometimes there will be small changes to get her to turn the water back on. Carol's job is to remain steadfast and communicate with responses like, "I felt really hurt when you did XYZ, and I don't feel like you are valuing me or that you really care about me." Carol must be careful not to get into any long discussions with her husband since that will feed his thirst for intimacy. She must wait for some serious long-term changes.

I remember another wonderful lady who did this but turned the water back on too soon. Her husband had moved out, then returned several weeks later wanting to make the marriage work. After several weeks, he said he couldn't do it and left again. She came back to my office and got back on track. Two months later, he came back again and made the radical changes she had hoped for.

Active-power people and passive-intimacy people. This is another common relational dynamic. An easy way of looking at this relationship is that one person is in the parent role and the other is the little child. This is typified by the mobster and the dumb blonde relationship. Most of the time, the passive-intimacy person is female and the active-power person is the male. The cornerstone of this dynamic is not based on intimacy but power. This relationship doesn't pivot on caring as does the previous relationship. This is more about control. The mobster, the active-power person, likes to control people. What better person to match with than the Marilyn-Monroe-type blonde who is looking for someone to be in charge of her life?

Unfortunately, in this dynamic there is often an absence of any caring, loving relationship. The passive-intimacy person is usually very happy to have someone buy a house or fur coat for her. The mobster isn't really looking for anybody to show care and empathy. He just wants someone he can control and who allows him to take what he wants. As we mentioned earlier, the active-power role is similar to that of Michael Corleone in "The Godfather." All of that power can be very attractive to someone who doesn't have much of their own.

Doris was a single mother just struggling to get by. She had found someone at work who was showing her all kinds of attention. He was sending her cards and calling her often. He found out what kind of flowers she liked and sent them to her office. "Boy, he must really love me," she thought. Soon he had bought her a very expensive ring and given it to her as a gesture of his "love" for her. Do you feel the quicksand closing in on Doris? She had confused control with love. Real love allows a person to cultivate his or her own power, not take it away. Doris was getting stuck in a relationship that looked more like a child with a parent than two adults. This relationship is destined for destruction. Doris and her boyfriend are both missing intimacy. Both will quickly feel stuck and miserable if the relationship doesn't change.

Another way of looking at this is the parent-child relationship that was covered earlier in the book. The person who is the power avoider is abdicating personal responsibility and inviting others to parent them. If the genders are reversed, it can be the lazy guy who cannot hold a job and doesn't help at all at home. The woman can be stuck being the over-responsible, codependent spouse who does everything. What tends to happen is that, initially, people see something attractive in a relationship, but it has an unhealthy component. Now they are trying to make it work. Once again, if there is something about me that needs fixing, I cannot find the answer in someone else. If I'm broken in some way, I am apt to find someone who fits my brokenness in an unhealthy way. Jesus said, "How can you say to your brother, 'Brother, let me take out the speck that is in your eye,' when you yourself do not see the log that is in your own eye? You hypocrite, first take the log out of your own eye, and then you will see clearly to take out the speck that is in your brother's eye" (Luke 6:42). I love this as a principle for life. Changing my world starts with changing myself. As I begin to be aware of my issues and weaknesses, I can better help deal with others and relationships.

Active-power people and active-power people. As unlikely as it may seem, I have seen this combination several times. In this type of relationship, both people are strong on power and weak on intimacy. What keeps them together is a mutual respect and admiration for each other. Both are somewhat comfortable without much caring or vulnerability. Both may be overachievers who enjoy drive and achievement.

Eventually, the relationship does not sustain. At some point, one or both of the partners is going to feel strain from the lack of bonding and commitment that comes with genuine intimacy. Many times when I work with these couples, there has been infidelity. It is very hard to have success in counseling in these situations because both partners are not usually the kind to be comfortable with vulnerability. They often want a quick fix or are looking to their partner for change. Both people must see the importance of generating intimacy and risk some vulnerability to make things better. This relational style might be seen in something like the old "I Love Lucy" show with Lucille Ball and Dezi Arnez. It also seems to be the style of what Howard Hughes and Katharine Hepburn had in their relationship.

Interactive power and intimacy individuals. It would be remiss if we didn't talk more about the healthy relationship. Interactive power and intimacy people are givers and receivers. P/I givers and receivers are people who have learned the secret of relational success. They are optimistic, caring, and growing. They do not have an attitude of avoiding others. They do not take from others—they receive. That is why I call them givers and receivers rather than givers and takers. There is a big difference. When someone receives, they are open to what someone else is offering them. Takers push or bully or manipulate. Receivers do not. They have learned that power and intimacy must come from within. Because they understand the need for both of these qualities in a healthy life, they look to foster them in themselves and others. That means that the relationship has respect for one another, along with caring and emotional giving.

Don and Rachel came into my office and quickly grabbed hold of the P/I formula. Before long, they were listening non-defensively to each other and sharing vulnerably. Both were open to learning new things about themselves and their partner to make their relationship better. Neither was looking to put the other down to build their own self-worth. At the same time, both were willing to share their own feelings and issues with the other because they saw their self-worth as coming from within themselves instead of their spouse. This couple was addressing issues right away before they built up and exploded because they cared for themselves as well as their relationship with each other.

The style of their conversations changed as well. Fewer questions were presented and more "I" statements were shared. Feelings were talked about more than empty facts. They were comfortable letting the other person share without interrupting. Don and Rachel were also able to stick to one subject at a time without deflecting the conversation. Most people deflect the topic onto something else as a defensive move to protect themselves. Because relationships are important to Don and Rachel, they were comfortable with a time-out policy. One only sacrifices for that which has worth. In Don and Rachel's eyes, the relationship was just as important as their own wants and needs. Therefore it was now important that their conversations were successful ones.

When I was first married, I drew a diagram of what I envisioned as a family structure. At the top of the page was me, the head of the family. I drew a line down and there was my wife Kimberly. Off to the side of Kimberly were lines going down to the children we were yet to have. It looked like a big Coke bottle. I showed this to my wife (boy did I have a lot of learning to do) and told her that this was my idea of our family hierarchy. She had grown up in a strong Christian family, and I was sure she would agree. Instead, she took a look at the diagram and said, "I don't agree with that." I asked her why and she said she thought she was my equal. That was startling. I couldn't see how that was going to work. I thought about that verse in 1 Corinthians that says, "But I want you to understand that Christ is the head of every man, and the man is the head of a woman, and God is the head of Christ" (1 Cor. 11:3).

The more I thought about headship, however, the more I considered the idea of a human head in relation to the body. I realized right away that the head needs the body and the body needs the head. They are one. The head is there to take care of the body. The head communicates with the body and looks to supply its needs. To me, that means leadership. I started thinking how the relational leadership of co-owners of a business works. If my children came to me as employees asking for a day off, could I make the decision? Of course I could. I'm the owner, but do I make the decision? Maybe I don't. Maybe out of respect for my partner, I tell my children that I will talk to mom and get back to them. Going to my wife isn't a lack of leadership. It *is* being the leader! Leaders communicate. That's part of leadership. Leadership includes communicating and making sure all the parts of the family are thriving. Now my idea of headship over a family has taken on more of the idea of caring and giving and mutuality than when I was newly married. My wife needs power and intimacy and so do my children. I am working harder at finding ways to help them reflect the design that God intended for them.

In the New Testament, Paul writes to Timothy, "For God has not given us a spirit of timidity, but of power and love and discipline (2 Tim. 1:7). I love that verse. These are the characteristics we have been talking about. The spirit we have from God encompasses power and intimacy (love) along with discipline. The Greek word for discipline here carries the idea of having a sound mind or self-control or moderation. As a therapist, I'm always looking to help people wanting a sound mind! I have five children, so I'm looking for it myself sometimes. What this verse says to me is that this power and intimacy formula is the lost key to helping us get that sound mind we all long for.

Power and intimacy givers and receivers are able to share their feelings and listen and care for the feelings of others. P/I givers are comfortable with respecting boundaries and understand the importance of free will. They are okay with compromise as well as sometimes giving up their own will for the sake or benefit of another. At the same time, they are strong enough to stand for things they believe in.

Know: We all have developed patterns of interaction. If patterns have been developed, they can also be improved.

Consider: Think of the ways you may increase power or intimacy to improve your relationships.

Do: Talk to someone close whom you trust about the relational patterns and ways you both may improve them.

Chapter 14

POWER AND INTIMACY IN PSYCHOLOGY

> "The fact is that people are good. Give people affection and security, and they will give affection and be secure in their feelings and their behavior."
> — Maslow

In the world of psychology, the DSM-IV is the diagnostic manual therapists use to help identify psychological issues faced by their patients. In this "bible" of psychotherapy, there is confirmation of the power-intimacy formula. Many of the diagnoses are connected to one or the other. Think of depression. Depression deals with loss. The loss of what? Most likely, the loss of power or intimacy or both. The same with anxiety. What are we usually anxious about? The *potential* loss of power or intimacy. Many mental disorders can easily be categorized as either dealing with power or intimacy issues.

In a power-intimacy continuum, some personality types can fall on either side of the equation. On the power side, people moving away from the center start off by being too selfish, judgmental, or critical of others. As they move further from the center, they become self-centered, manipulative, and narcissistic. If they continue, they can become avoidant or sociopathic. Moving in the opposite direction from the center towards intimacy, people can become too enabling, passive, and people-pleasing. If they keep going, they can become histrionic or dependent.

POWER

sociopath/avoidant-narcissistic-selfish

GOOD BOUNDARIES

enabling-passive-dependent

INTIMACY

One's power-intimacy continuum is not always exclusive. In borderline personality disorder, people continually flip-flop to both sides of the continuum. Borderline personality disorder is an attempt to find a balance of power and intimacy, but because such people have been severely wounded emotionally, they slingshot from one end of the spectrum to the other. They are in such emotional pain that they cannot handle the middle ground for long. They cannot tolerate the mild wounding and potential wounding that a healthy balance involves. It is like dealing with such a sunburn that even the gentlest touch of another is too painful. Growing up in South Florida, I would often get very painful sunburns. My mother would try to help by putting cream on my back. Yow! It was always cold and very difficult to tolerate. Even though she was trying to love me, I couldn't handle it. Thanks, mom! You can think of borderline personality disorder as being something like that.

In the story "The Christmas Carol," Scrooge learned the importance of finding this balance. Scrooge had become an avoidant, grouchy old grump. But he was starving for intimacy. He could have paid for intimacy with his money, but he knew that was not going to satisfy him. He longed for genuine intimacy—the kind that is found when people care for one another. He saw that in his journeys with the different ghosts of Christmas. The ghost of Christmas past reminded him of his old friend Fezziwig, who treated others with sincerity and kindness, and the young lady, Belle, who had offered him a chance for true intimacy. The ghost of Christmas present allowed him to see the love of the Cratchit family and his own nephew, Fred. Scrooge longed to rebalance his life and add intimacy. The fears of Christmas future propelled him to find the courage to be vulnerable. Thankfully, the story has a happy ending: "He went to church, and walked about the streets, and watched the people hurrying to and fro, and patted children on the head, and questioned beggars, and looked down into the kitchens of houses, and up to the windows, and found that everything could yield him pleasure. He had never dreamed that any walk—that anything—could give him so much happiness."

When I look at my graduate work in psychology, my mentor was right. My research is filled with wonderful tools about human nature, and true to my mentor's word, most of it could fall under the umbrellas of power and intimacy. Many of the stage theorists focus on the accomplishment of personal empowerment (power) and social connections (intimacy). Freud, with his stage development, focused on independence and trust. The same could be said of Erickson with his stages of development. Some of the different stages that Erickson covered dealt with trust, autonomy, initiative, industry, and intimacy. All of those fit under the power/intimacy formula. Alfred Adler, a contemporary of Freud, was a strong proponent of empowerment and developed the idea of the inferiority complex.

In more recent years, the development of attachment theory has been a powerful and useful tool as well. Attachment theory, first postulated by John Bowlby, focuses on the importance of children having adult attachment figures during their developmental years to help them grow into healthy adults. Children who do not have healthy attachments can have very insecure relationships as they get older and those relationships can quickly move into "fight or flight." It is critical that they find healthy attachments when they are young so they grow up having the benefits of developing healthy balance of power and intimacy. Otherwise they can develop major emotional and psychological problems that push them away from the balanced formula and cause them to tilt to one extreme or the other.

If we look at power and intimacy as a spectrum, we see that in the middle the individual is in a healthy state. If an individual does not get a healthy balance of attachment, he can move toward one end of the spectrum or the other. I believe the direction people will go is dictated by whether they find attachment or rejection within the unhealthy bonding. If people find attachment within the unhealthy bonding of a high-power person, they will move toward the extreme power side of the equation—they can find themselves on the side of becoming selfish or narcissistic. If they do not find attachment but rejection from the extreme power person, they will move toward the intimacy extreme. Conversely, if children find attachment and approval from an extremely intimate person, they can become extremely intimate—enabling, passive, and dependent. If children find rejection of that connection, they will move toward the power extreme of the continuum, becoming avoidant or narcissistic. Therefore it is important for an individual to receive that balance of power and intimacy as they develop.

More recently, this idea has been adapted to adult interactions and social patterns. Cindy Hazan and Phillip Shaver identify several different patterns: securely attached, anxious-preoccupied, dismissive-avoidant, and fearful-avoidant. Wikipedia gives a nice explanation of these different patterns. In its section on attachment theory, it states: "Securely attached adults tend to have positive views of themselves, their partners and their relationships. They feel comfortable with intimacy and independence, balancing the two." You may notice that this definition specifically touches on the balance of intimacy and independence, or again, our formula for power and intimacy. Anxious-preoccupied adults, on the other hand, "seek high levels of intimacy, approval and responsiveness from partners, becoming overly dependent. They tend to be less trusting, have less positive views about themselves and their partners, and may exhibit high levels of emotional expressiveness, worry, and impulsiveness in their relationships." Here is the overly intimate side of the equation. Dismissive-avoidant adults are similarly unbalanced. They desire a high level of independence, often appearing to avoid attachment altogether. They view themselves as self-sufficient, invulnerable to attachment feelings, and not needing close relationships. They tend to suppress their feelings, dealing with rejection by distancing themselves from partners of whom they often have a poor opinion (there's the tilted power person like Scrooge!). "Fearful-avoidant adults have mixed feelings about close relationships, both desiring and feeling uncomfortable with emotional closeness. They tend to mistrust their partners and view themselves as unworthy." There is the flip-flop we previously mentioned. Humans can move into one side or the other of the spectrum. Anxious-preoccupied adults are too far on the intimacy spectrum, becoming dependent, whereas dismissive-avoidant and fearful-avoidant adults have gone to the power side of the equation to avoid intimacy.

Look at Maslow's hierarchy of needs and again the formula resurfaces. Maslow states that we have need basic needs of existence and safety (power). Once those needs are met, we humans need things like love and belonging (intimacy). Further up Maslow's hierarchy is self-esteem and esteem by others. These easily plug into the P/I formula for our needs.

In essence, what we must do to be happy is find a way to live that promotes both power and intimacy. We must resist the temptation to do anything that promotes one at the cost of another. This is critical. There are some power behaviors that will increase our power but reduce (sometimes radically) our intimacy at the same time. There are some intimacy behaviors that will increase our intimacy but reduce (sometimes radically) our power at the same time. So here is a very easy formula for healthy living: Find behaviors that promote both.

Know: Both spiritual and mental health is based on a healthy balance of power and intimacy.

Consider: Think about your life and consider your power and intimacy "diet" growing up.

Do: Pick an area of work in your own life to improve your power and intimacy needs.

Chapter 15

POWER AND INTIMACY IN PARENTING

"Your mother died to save you. If there is one thing Voldemort cannot understand, it is love. He didn't realize that love as powerful as your mother's for you leaves its own mark. Not a scar, no visible sign . . . to have been loved so deeply, even though the person who loved us is gone, will give us some protection forever." — Dumbledore ("Harry Potter")

What an exciting thought! Love is a powerful force. In the Harry Potter series, we have Tom Riddle scared of death and longing for a power strong enough to overcome it. Tom was trying hard to use dark magic, while Harry used the power of love. Throughout the series the classic battle wages, the power of love is ultimately stronger than anything Tom Riddle can find.

I could not go throughout this book without commenting on love. Healthy love is really only expressed within the balance of power and intimacy. The people too far over on the intimacy side of the equation do not really value or love their own selves. Their love is usually not selfless but has some self-seeking goal to it. Perhaps it is a desire for others to love back and confirm they are loveable. People on the power side do not really value or love others either. They only want others to love them as well. Healthy love comes from someone who values and loves himself and values and loves another. This is found nowhere better than in parenting. Healthy parenting is teaching children to love and respect themselves and their neighbors. Knowing that my child needs power and intimacy in his or her life to build self-worth sets the foundation for all I do as a parent.

One of my favorite books on parenting is a paperback by Kenneth Kaye called *Family Rules*. One of the main ideas is that both consequences and rewards are important for raising children. Let's first start with the power side of the equation. It is interesting that both consequences and rewards directly build our power. The child who has rewards and consequences clearly sees his impact on others and the environment. Just imagine if Adam and Eve had tasted of the tree of good and evil and nothing happened. What if God had said to them, "Oh, you must not have understood me clearly. Let me give you another chance." Then they failed again. What if God had come back several times and given allowances? Maybe one time he said, "Oh, darn, I put the tree in the *middle* of the garden. That was my fault. Let's try it again and I'll put it way out in the back forty." What would success and failure have felt like? It would have been a very empty feeling. No matter what you did, it wouldn't seem to matter. The result would be that you would feel powerless. I don't know about you, but I don't like feeling powerless. I imagine our children don't like it much either.

It always interested me that in the story of Adam and Eve, they got one shot at failure. There were no second chances. One would think that God might have offered a do-over. After all, consider the consequences. We're talking death and disease and sickness to mankind here. I grew up playing a little golf and I always had mixed feelings about the mulligan, which is essentially a do-over. It seemed to taint the whole golf experience. If you give one person a do-over, why not give him two? Then three? When I was a little guy about twelve, I played in a golf tournament for children. I remember a child in front of us hitting his golf ball out of bounds. He got very angry, started cussing, and threw one of his clubs. Then he walked back towards the clubhouse. I remember an official picking him up in a golf cart and driving him back to the hole he was on and letting him continue to play. From that point on, the whole tournament didn't feel fair. In a way, I've begun to see that, in the garden of Eden, God wanted us to know our decisions are important. *We* are important. Of course, there is another lesson here that is hard for us humans to understand. Man had just crossed over from sinless light to sinful dark. God could not let sin live eternally. Once we crossed into that sinful state, that sinful state would have to die.

So one important thing that we can do to help our children is to make sure they feel the effect of their choices and behaviors. The more we can be there to help them experience true rewards and consequences, the more we are helping them with their self-worth. Parenting is a lot like teaching children to ride a bike. In an effort to help them learn, we hold onto the handlebars and the seat. Our children feel powerful as they see what they can accomplish with our support. At some point, we have to let go or they are never going to learn to ride on their own. The parent who comes out with her child and just gives her a bike before going back inside is too uninvolved. On the other extreme is the parent who holds onto the bike the whole time and never gives the child a chance to learn on his own. Healthy empowerment is a weaning off support as our children show competency.

Kenneth Kaye went on to explain that there are two types of natural consequences, logical consequences and arbitrary consequences. What a wonderful idea to let natural consequences apply unless they are too damaging (like getting run over by a car). Then we must kick in logical consequences. Kaye is basically saying that in the grown-up world when we don't go to work for several weeks, our boss doesn't come take our cars away. That would be illogical. We get fired! As parents, we want our children to learn this principle. I see these logical consequences as falling into one of three areas all starting with the letter "p": possessions, privileges, and people time. I try to match the punishment with the crime. If it involves a possession, I'll take the possession away. If it involves privileges, then I take a privilege away. Arbitrary is just whatever seems to work. Being that I'm only human, I will use that one often.

Another wonderful tool I love from his book is the "if-then" principle. This again promotes the importance of power in our children's lives. When my children were little, I found myself nagging until I would pop a cork. I might have asked my son to get off the computer and go clean his room. When it wouldn't happen, I would ask over and over until I started yelling—or sometimes begging! Then I started using Kenneth Kaye's "if-then" principle. Instead of threatening and repeating, I began declaring the rewards and consequences. I would tell my son, "If you don't get off the computer and head on upstairs by the time I count to ten, then you will lose XYZ." Then I'd stick to it. How wonderful that my children started to get power and self-worth instead of a dose of anger. Using the "if-then" principle also helped me decide on a consequence or reward while I was calm. It is like football. The offense gets into a huddle and calls a play while everything is calm. Then when the ball is hiked and everything is going crazy, the players know what to do. The same applies to parenting. I would create a consequence or reward while I was calm, then when I got frustrated with my children's lack of obedience, I would just follow the play I'd already called. Kenneth Kaye has a whole chapter on escalating, and he makes a good point that we should start with the least amount of discipline so we can escalate later if we need to do so.

I also found that there were times when I would dole out consequences and my children would react poorly. Sometimes they would yell and scream and kick something. I would have to discipline that, too. Then they would go off again and I would have to discipline that, too. All of a sudden, my children were in control and I was escalating until I couldn't follow through. Has this ever happened to you? To counteract that, I started using two "if-then" principles. I would use one for the action and one for the possible reaction. I would tell my daughter, "If you don't get off the computer and go clean up your room, then you will lose your phone the rest of the night. If you throw a fit, kick, or scream or show any other bad response, then I can take it away for longer." I would also tell them that I could keep going, too, but I'd rather not. This would let my children know that I have the bases covered. My goal was to keep things from escalating in a negative direction. I wanted to keep the fire in the campground and not start a forest fire!

I used to give the children positive consequence for their discipline as well. What do I mean by that? Some consequences take things away. That would be a simple negative (as in subtraction) consequence. There is also the opportunity to follow that with a positive consequence (addition). Usually this would be in the form of earning something they just lost. As an example, when my son did something wrong, I might take his Xbox away for a week. That would be a simple negative consequence. To change that to a positive, I would add something that could hasten the Xbox's return. What might that be? For some parents, it might be a list of chores. I prefer to look at character. I want to effectively add to my children's power and intimacy. This area is often overlooked. One time my son got really angry at one of his four sisters and I wanted him to realize the importance of not letting anger rule our lives. (I have to give him a little compassion since he is one boy with four sisters). I told him he was going to lose his Xbox until he could recite a Bible verse of my choosing. The verse was Proverbs 16:32: "He who is slow to anger is better than the mighty, and he who rules his spirit, than he who captures a city." Let's just say that he was highly motivated to memorize that verse! I had to laugh at how hard he worked to memorize it. Maybe you have seen that with your own children.

Another helpful tool I've used is a positive consequence I call the "buy back" plan. Many times when children are disciplined, they begin to feel powerless and hopeless. This is a very dangerous time when children can become more destructive because they have "nothing to lose." To help our children feel more power, I would give them a chance to earn back whatever they had lost in half the time. That would get their interest up. So they would ask, "So how do I get it back?" and I would tell them I was going to measure their attitude every day. Many times, we give our children chores to earn back whatever they've lost. But if their attitudes are terrible, what does that really accomplish? This is where the intimacy side of the equation comes in. Now they are seeing the power of relationships in their lives. Our children were learning that fixing relationships gives them things! Relationships are powerful! I would tell them that I was going to monitor their hearts or attitudes every day. If their attitudes were more than halfway good, they would pass. I wouldn't make my decision until the whole day was over. That way, if they had a bad morning but a good rest of the day, they might just get a passing grade.

You can tailor the terms of the "buy back" plan to the age of the children. Young children will do fine with green for pass and red for fail. I let our children know that whether they passed or failed was totally my decision but they didn't have much of an argument because I was only asking for more than halfway. That's hardly negotiable! Every passing day took one day off their discipline. One day for one day. Thus, they could get things back in half the time. What's really clever about this is if you know you are going to allow them to do a buy back, you can make the discipline time a little longer to adjust for it and nobody is the wiser! Your child thinks he or she is a hero and you end up giving them the discipline you think they deserve!

A very easy way to monitor this is to use a simple wall calendar. Make sure you write down the discipline on the day you start so there is no arguing about the start date (in case you have a son like mine). I might put something like, "No Xbox /10 days." Then I only mark off the failed days and don't put anything down for the pass days. That way sometimes I don't mark anything at all. Now my children are the ones coming to me asking how they're doing! The plan runs itself! You may, of course, have a bad day that has to require more discipline than simply an X on the calendar. That's fine. Just make sure you use something different and keep this going on course. It is important for children to feel that they are still going to earn something back. By the way, we need them to earn things back so we can take them away again!

Once you use this buy back plan, you may find the same plan useful to help your children earn things as well. Children want things, and if you're like me you start asking yourself, "Why am I giving my children something when they have such a bad attitude?" Now we can use the same attitude tool. I would tell my children we are going to use the same red/green tool to earn what they want. Sometimes I would tie it to a monetary value. I might ask them how much the object they want is. They might say $30. I tell them every passing or green day, I will contribute

X amount of money towards that goal. For instance, if I chose $1 a day, they would have to give me 30 passing days. I used this idea with a mother several years ago to help her child go to summer camp. Her daughter was so difficult that she did not let her daughter go to camp the year before. Her daughter really wanted to go to camp the following year, so we set up a goal for her to earn the $50 she needed for a down payment. Then we set up a plan for her to earn the remaining $300. We also allowed for some possible fail days. You know what? Her daughter went to camp!

Some clients have said they don't feel it is right for their children to get paid for having a good attitude. To these I ask, "What do you pay your children for?" Some say things like mowing the lawn or washing the car. I would ask my clients which has more value. I also ask them to think about how much they have paid in counseling to help their child with their attitudes? Children are now learning the importance of intimacy!

Now let's take a further look at the intimacy side of parenting. It is important that our children think about others and not just themselves. One of the things that I never liked growing up was the feeling of isolation that can arise when we do wrong. Sometimes parents get angry when their children disobey. We give them a consequence and tell them it is over, but we still walk around all day upset and frustrated. What a self-worth killer. Children can begin to think that intimacy is impossible. They can begin at an early age to dislike relationships and find them painful. I suspect this is exactly how Adam and Eve felt when they hid themselves from the presence of God. How wonderful that God made garments of skin and clothed Adam and Eve so they could come back out into the open. This is a wonderful gesture of reconnection. Wouldn't it be great if we could discipline our children, give them consequences, and then it is over? Once my children receive their consequence, I want to make sure they feel reconnected and loved. I want to make sure I leave any bad feelings behind so my children can feel the joy of intimacy.

Another tool I have used to build intimacy between siblings is making sure they reconnect with any of their brothers and sisters they may have wronged. In our family, the wording is, "I'm sorry, would you forgive me?" That extra little, "Would you forgive me?" is a wonderful phrase to help with humility. If they don't use that phrase, there is more of a consequence. Sometimes the other sibling will say, "I don't want to forgive him." We would make our children do it or they would get a consequence as well. Intimacy is important in our family and we wanted them to realize it. Of course, there were times when I would get too angry with them and they would go up into their rooms. They knew what was coming. I had to lead by example. I went in to my children and said that same wonderful phrase, "I'm sorry, would you forgive me?"

I remember a wonderful learning experience about teaching our children about the value of intimacy and how they have the power to damage it. It was when my son was thirteen years old. We had disciplined him for something and he got upset, swore under his breath, and threw some things, and then slammed a door. I remember Kimberly going in to calm him down and help him verbalize his feelings. She would talk him through his feelings and try to change his thinking. All that sounds pretty wonderful. Unfortunately, he kept doing more angry things. One time, he said if we were going to take his Xbox away, then he might as well kill himself. Kimberly went in to calm him down and talk through his feelings again. Sounds good to me. But he continued to threaten to harm himself. Kimberly came to me and we stood back and tried to look at our situation. We did not realize it, but we were giving thirty wonderful minutes of positive attention for negative behavior. We were reinforcing the very actions we were trying to change. We changed our game plan. We told him we were waiting for an apology (with a humble heart). Until then, Kimberly and I were going to be cold and distant. Intimacy had been broken. Jordan would come out and say, "Hey mom, what's for breakfast?" We would just respond with a short, "Eggs and we're waiting for an apology." I would pick him up from Pop Warner and he would start talking to me about practice and ask to go to his favorite food spot. I would respond with a short, "No, we're going home, and I'm waiting for an apology." He just refused and looked out the side window all the way home. Stubborn little guy! It was cold in our household, and it was tough for my wife and me. We did not enjoy it, and we almost caved in. On the fifth day, Jordan came to mom and said, "Mom, can I talk to you for a second?' My wife said, "Sure, Jordan, what's up?" He said to mom, "Mom, I'm sorry for yelling and slamming the door, would you forgive me?" Mom said yes, of course. They hugged. Then my son said something to her I'll never forget. He said, "Mom that was killing me. This is the best I've ever felt!" We never saw that coming. He went out and had the best Pop Warner practice he's ever had. He apologized to me as well.

You know what? We saw a major reduction in his negative behavior after that. He got negative attention for negative behavior and positive attention for positive behavior. My son learned the value of intimacy. My saying from all that is, "Whoever burns a bridge has to rebuild the bridge." I cannot rebuild a bridge that someone else has burned. I cannot take that joy away from them!

When our children were growing up, we kept an eye out for this delicate balance between power and intimacy. At one point, we felt that activities were getting in the way of family unity. With five children, we had to cut back to help them stay united and feel that the family was a valuable component of their lives. This was balancing the power side with the intimacy side for our children.

Of course, another fun thing that many of us do is have a family night. We used to choose Sunday night since the children were getting ready for school the next day. It worked out wonderfully. We would vary our content to keep family nights fun. Sometimes we would read through a book. Other times we would just play a game. Sometimes we would read through a book in the Bible. The point was that we were together as family, building memories.

Another way to build this power and intimacy connection is the parent's type of relationship with their children. A parent really uses two hats while raising children. One is the role of a parent and the other is the role of a friend. When children are little, we are mostly a parent, more in charge of them than anything else. When our children are grown with children of their own, we are mostly their friends. In the teenage years, we're juggling both roles. This is exactly the power and intimacy formula. Being in charge of our children, doling out consequences, demonstrates the power side of life to our relationships. Being their friend brings out the intimacy. We know some parents who are too much of a friend to their children. They might go drink beer with their teenage son or participate in some other unhealthy behavior. Then there are parents who are never their children's friends. Their approach is cold, distant parenting with no human element. Mixing both hats of parent and friend (or mixing power and intimacy) is just the right formula.

Another of my favorite verses in the Bible is, "By loving kindness and truth iniquity is atoned for, and by the fear of the Lord one keeps away from evil" (Prov. 16:6). What a perfect example of power and intimacy with God. The first part of that verse is the intimacy side of the equation—loving kindness and truth. The loving kindness comes from God, and the truth is a heart of a repentant sinner. All of that creates atonement for iniquity. Then the verse goes on to say it is by the fear of the Lord that keeps us from evil. That is the power side of God, which speaks of his judgment. This perfect blend of power and intimacy keeps us healthy before God. It is the same thing with our children. We want them to enjoy both aspects, which is why my wife and I try to give them a healthy, balanced life.

Know: Children also need power and intimacy to be successful and emotionally healthy.

Consider: Think of ways you may have inadvertently not promoted power and intimacy in your child's life.

Do: Employ some of these tools to help increase your child's power and intimacy.

Chapter 16

POWER AND INTIMACY IN ADDICTIONS

"Here's to alcohol: the cause of—and solution to—all of life's problems."

— Homer Simpson

Many times people come into my office frustrated and confused because they have been stuck in some addiction and don't understand why they cannot break free of it. As a cognitive-behavioral therapist, I am always looking for tools to help. I love the addiction cycle developed by Dr. Robert Hemfelt, Dr. Frank Minirth, and Dr. Paul Meier in their book *Love Is a Choice*. In it, they discuss how many of us have a love bucket that can become empty at times. When it does, we will start looking for an "anesthetic" to ease the pain. As we go along, that choice gives us relief. Unfortunately, it can also give us consequences. Sometimes these consequences cause us to have guilt and shame. Of course, that drains our bucket even more, so we go back out and do the same thing again to try to fill it up. So the cycle continues.

As I have used the power and intimacy formula to help my clients, I have wondered if it could be applied to the cycle of addiction. Of course, it can. If power and intimacy are the building blocks of self-worth, then this formula should help people fill their self-worth buckets back up.

Every addiction can fit into the power and intimacy formula. Every addiction has an attraction that seems to increase our power or our intimacy or both. Let's pick a common one—drinking. When people decide to go out on Friday night, what are they looking for? Often they are looking for a way to forget about their problems. If we don't have any problems, we feel empowered! Drinking is a way to add power to our powerless situations. When we go to the bar, we also socialize and have fun times—intimacy. Now we have someone trying to find ways to increase their power and intimacy. Sound familiar? What about those people who stay home alone and just drink the night

129

away? They're looking for empowerment alone. Most likely, they are tilted to the power side of the equation. Many times that's someone high on power feeling depressed with life's constant drain.

Next, let's look at overeating. That's one of my struggles. I love to go to the store and buy tons of food to stock up in my house. You know why? It makes me feel safe and secure. I have everything I need for several days. I have enough milk and paper towels . . . I feel empowered. I also love to go out to eat. Eating out with my family is very social. It is intimacy! The same thing could be applied to someone who shops too much. It also holds true with pornography or sex with a prostitute. There is empowerment in the idea that someone is going to take off their clothes and do vulnerable things, whether on film or in reality. If it is pornography, the viewer is in control (empowerment). If it is a call girl, she does whatever she is paid to do. Of course, in the mind of some, there is intimacy (although this is really a false intimacy) as well. In the mind of the viewer or the John, there is a shared vulnerability or intimacy. Again we have the formula at work.

Another is gambling. I remember Mark. He was one of my first clients. He came to me because his gambling addiction was destroying the family. He was a Christian with a wife and two small children. He told me that he used to be a really good motocross professional. He would go around the country with other riders on the circuit and compete, then one day he hit his head and could no longer race competitively. Now he was stuck in a dead-end job he didn't like. His dream was gone. He had a tremendous drop of power and intimacy and would go play poker because he enjoyed the competition. He also liked the possibility of getting good at something at which he could also make money (power). I asked him, "Is there any other reason why you go to the casino?" He said, "Well, yes, it is the same people every Saturday. We really have a good time" (intimacy).

Workaholism is another common addiction. Someone who goes to work gets a lot of empowerment and usually enjoys some social connection. If you look at it in terms of addiction, they work to help increase their self-worth or power and intimacy. Work gives them relief in one area, but they might neglect their family and marriage and suffer consequences. That causes shame and guilt, lowering their self-worth. So where do they go tomorrow? Back to work.

If you can think of any addiction, you can probably find some drive for power or intimacy or both. Even in codependency, people are often using other people to fill up their buckets. By meeting someone else's needs or taking care of them, there can be a feeling of intimacy or empowerment.

How can this knowledge help people change their lives? Sir Francis Bacon said, "Knowledge is power." Self awareness is the beginning of healing. With knowledge and self-awareness, I am prepared for change. There's nothing like x-rays with cancer spots to get me ready to quit smoking. The first thing I must do to break that cycle is find something better at the top of the circle that will fulfill my need for power and intimacy. With the P/I formula, we know why we do the things we do. There are much better choices to increase my power and intimacy. Going to the gym increases my power and can increase my intimacy without having a negative consequence. Joining some clubs can bring intimacy and power, too. Going to church also brings us both power and intimacy.

Another helpful way to stop draining the self-worth bucket has to do with the shame and guilt aspect of the addiction cycle. There are many different ideas about the difference between shame and guilt. I have come to embrace one that looks at guilt as an external issue. If I took $5 from you that you left on my desk, I would feel guilty about that. Let's make that guilt a focus on the action, not the person. The action was wrong. I could be troubled about that until I finally gave it back to you. Guilt—which is external—can be a healthy thing. It tells me that an action I did was wrong. Shame, on the other hand, is internal. To me, shame has no healthy benefit. Shame internalizes guilt and makes it about the person, not the action. "I'm a bad person." "I hate myself." An example of the difference between the two can be found in the New Testament when Peter denied Christ. He didn't just deny Christ once. Peter denied him three times, and he was deeply troubled. When Peter saw Jesus on the beach after his resurrection, he jumped from the boat and swam for shore. He couldn't wait to make things right. Let's call that guilt "godly sorrow" (2 Chron. 7:11). Judas Iscariot had guilt, too. He betrayed Jesus, but then he hung himself. That is shame. Judas hated himself so much that all he could do was kill himself. I tell my clients to stay with healthy guilt and avoid dangerous shame that depletes your love bucket and makes you more susceptible to destructive tendencies.

One of my favorite books is *Failing Forward* by John Maxwell. I appreciate his approach to failure as an external and not an internal issue. That is the wonderful beauty of the Christian message. We are loved for who we are, not what we do. As an example, Dave was a young Christian guy who came into my office during a college break. He was feeling down and depressed. One of the things he was dealing with was a sense of failure. He kept telling me he wanted to do some major thing in his life to start over and clean the slate. He had thought about jumping off a bridge overlooking a lake as a way to do that. I couldn't help but smile. When I was a lot younger, I remember thinking the same thing. Dave had gotten tangled up in loads of shame. I shared the cycle addiction can bring as well as the difference between guilt and shame.

Long ago, I was deeply troubled by my sin and felt frustration and shame, too. One morning I was driving down the freeway so consumed by my failure that I hardly noticed a woman and a young boy on the side of the freeway. Their car wasn't working. This was before cell phones, and I almost drove right by. As I did, it hit me between the eyes that I was so busy with my own weaknesses that I was no good to others. I remember feeling as if God were saying to me, "John, I died on the cross for your moral weaknesses. Let it go and start loving others!" It was as if I had been spending all my time focusing on the weeds in my life that I had no time left to plant flowers! I pulled that car around and bought the mother and her son some orange juice and a roll and asked if they needed some help. "Above all, keep fervent in your love for one another, because love covers a multitude of sins" (1 Peter 4:8). Who knew that one act of kindness and love could cover many of our own moral failures?

If we keep working on planting flowers in our lives, they will choke out the weeds. If I focus solely on pulling weeds, all I might end up with is dirt! Christ died for our weeds so that we might plant flowers! The Christian life is all about daily having to come to God and allow him to clean our slates.

I told Dave that if he felt he had to jump off of some bridge to clean his slate, he would have to jump off a lot of bridges. I encouraged him to accept the daily task of letting God do the slate-cleaning and get busy focusing on loving others instead. Many of us are familiar with that passage in the Bible in which Jesus is washing the disciples' feet. Years ago, I heard a sermon in which the pastor discusses how Peter did not think it was right for Jesus to wash his feet. Jesus replies, "If I do not wash you, you have no part with Me" (John 13:8). Peter then says, "Lord, then wash not only my feet, but also my hands and my head." Give me a bath! Jesus tells Peter that he has already been cleansed and only needs to have his feet washed. Every day, Peter will get his feet dirty. Every day, he will have to get his feet cleansed. My encouragement to David was to accept this truth and make it part of his daily life.

It isn't fun having to acknowledge our need for cleansing every day. But it keeps us humble. By keeping his wrong external—by keeping it about his behavior and not his person—David was able to keep his internal love tank full. This approach kept him from possibly returning to the very destructive thing he thought would fill his tank to begin with. David was able to poison his destructive thoughts and render them powerless by focusing on planting flowers. By normalizing the process of breaking and restoring fellowship, he was able to add positive loving acts.

Know: Every addiction is an attempt to increase our power or intimacy.

Consider: Think of areas in your life in which you may have tried to increase your power or intimacy in an unhealthy way.

Do: Refuse to get caught up in unhealthy shame when you do something wrong. Instead, stay with healthy guilt.

CONCLUSION

"Do not rejoice over me, O my enemy. Though I fall I will rise; though I dwell in darkness, the Lord is a light for me." (Micah 7:8)

Micah 7:8 is one of my all-time favorite verses. In it, there is such a determination to continue to do good things regardless of the defeat in one's life. This is not encouragement to do evil, but to do good.

This book has been written for you and your relationships. The idea of the power and intimacy formula is very simple but effective. I have seen many clients leave my office with new insights on the purpose of life. The wonderful thing about this formula is that it can be just as useful in its simplicity as in its more detailed form. From this idea, we can see what we need to be happy in life and in our relationships—power and intimacy. We also know that others need this to be happy, too. We cannot just live by power or intimacy alone and hope to get the other from someone else. We must have both in our lives to be fulfilled.

Another wonderful principle of the P/I formula is that it gives each of us the power to change our world. As we rebalance our lives, it causes others to feel some dissonance relationally with us, but in a good way. This promotes healthy relationships. The more you come into contact with people when you are in a healthy, balanced state, the more they will be drawn to be balanced in return. You and I have a mission to help this world by simply helping ourselves. By doing so, you and I can be the salt of the earth and a light to the world.

Made in the USA
San Bernardino, CA
11 February 2017